Sea Of Green

The Perpetual Harvest

HIGH TIMES Books

Printed in the U.S.A.

ISBN # 0-9647858-1-1

Written by: "Hans"
and Tina Wright
Editor: John Holmstrom
Consulting Editor: Max Yields
Copy Editors: Gabe Kirchheimer, Marina Zogbi, Steve Wishnia
Editorial Assistant: Mark Siegel

Cover and Interior Design: Erik-Loren Council
Illustrations by John Decamillis
Cover photograph by Andre Grossmann
All other photographs by "Hans" (except where noted)

First edition: March 1998

Dedication

This book is dedicated to my eight children.
I see their smiling faces.
They are the light through which truth shines.
They are the truth through which light shines.

"Dad"

Section One
GENERAL INFORMATION

contents

Section Two
THE SEA OF GREEN METHOD

AUTHOR'S NOTE

The "Sea of Green" is a marijuana-growing method primarily based on manipulating the photoperiod of very young clones that are grown quickly and efficiently, then "forced" into flowering and harvested. The name "Sea of Green" is derived from the fact that when viewed, the crop looks like a green sea, with wave after wave of buds ready for harvest.

The first to develop and popularize this concept was The Super Sativa Seed Club (S.S.S.C.), a superb group of growers in Holland. They developed the process in the 1980s and thereby turned marijuana-growing into a science and an art. The S.S.S.C. (which became defunct in the early 1990s) depended upon state-of-the-art electronics, modern greenhouse techniques and hydroponic (water-based) agricultural methods, but over the years their techniques have been modified by indoor growers in America. What I have dubbed the "Sea of Green" method is a simplified version of those advancements.

The basic concept of determining gender early and forcing plants to flower early has its roots as far as 1893, when the British government commissioned the first-ever study of cannabis use in India. This multi-volume report, published by the Indian Hemp Drugs Commission, was a scientific study of the effect of hashish use on the Indian people. It analyzed the variations in strength and effect of local product on people throughout all of India, and interviews with people whose fathers and grandfathers were growers were conducted for research purposes.

According to the Indian Hemp Drugs Commission Report, throughout Indian culture there have been people employed as "Plant Doctors" for many centuries who are able (among other things) to determine the sex of marijuana plants very early in their development. Plant Doctors would be called to the marijuana crops at a certain time in the plant's growth, and would look for certain pre-flowers that form the nodes of female plants. Due to their keen insight, these doctors could distinguish the hard-to-identify female bracts from the male pre-flowers. Once the females had been identified, the male plants would be pulled before they could develop and pollinate the females. This is the earliest reference in history to sinsemilla, which uninformed people think of as a product of "high-tech growing" but which obviously was already the result of an ancient practice in the 1800s.

It was also a long-standing practice of some Indian growers to place a clay pot over the tops of small females they knew to be of a superior breed. By reducing the light period each day, the plant would go to the flowering stage early. Sometimes the clay pot would be allowed to remain on the plant even when it was well into flowering. This final extended period of darkness would, it was believed, increase potency. Once the clay pot was removed, one side effect was that the plant had turned almost pure white because of the lack of sunlight.

While this is by no means the Sea Of Green method, it's similar to the basic concept. While marijuana growing methods from the past have been lost to history, it is a known fact that marijuana has been used for thousands of years by people all over the world, and many of today's so-called high-tech cultivation techniques are merely replications or improvements on centuries-old traditions.

It is estimated that hundreds of millions of people around the world now use marijuana in some form to obtain the pleasant effect it has to offer. If you do this in the United States of America, you must necessarily be involved in a form of civil disobedience. In order to obtain marijuana, you will have to either buy it or grow it in what are most often considered illegal endeavors. Since these transactions sometimes involve money flowing out of America, the patriotic thing to do would be to allow everyone to grow their own, in the privacy of their own homes.

Well, don't you know—here is a process which will allow you to do just that. So get off your butts, Daughters of the American Revolution: follow Betsy Ross's lead. All you old vets, stop telling those old, worn-out war stories and arm yourself with seeds and soil, and do the patriotic thing. Grow, grow, grow.

-Hans
Tin Alley

Disclaimer: We do not advocate the growing of bad marijuana.
So please, grow the good stuff.

INTRODUCTION

The Sea of Green is a specialized, mass-production technique for growing marijuana indoors in which the time required to bring your crop to harvest is shortened by controlling the light period. All aspects of the plant's life are controlled so that the shortest amount of time is taken to produce the largest amount of product in the least amount of space and a minimal amount of work.

We have developed this process into the "cottage industry" of marijuana-growing techniques. That is because we have fashioned the process to be easily accomplished by the average person, using common, standard items and equipment.

The process is best done indoors, and you may do it on any scale you wish. (The technique won't change.) If you wish to grow only a small closet's worth, that's fine. If one wishes to grow a room-sized crop, that's fine too. If you wish to grow a factory-size crop, the process is still the same. [*Editor's Note: Keep in mind that federal sentencing guidelines call for a mandatory minimum of five years for cultivation of 100 or more plants, and that each clone, cutting, and seedling will be counted as a full plant.*]

The Sea of Green method may be used in a basement, an attic, an outbuilding, a portable trailer or virtually any unused space. You will be limited only by your imagination and creativity. The season doesn't interfere either; you can grow during the winter or summer (although some heat or air conditioning might be required).

One of the greatest aspects of this process is that you can determine when you want to harvest. You can harvest once a week, once every two weeks or once every three weeks. The decision is yours. Once the harvest starts, it is self-perpetuating. Week after week, wave after wave of female buds, you'll be harvesting a virtual sea of green.

Another dynamic aspect of the process is the 18" to 22" single-stalk bud. The growing of all non-essential parts of the marijuana plant is eliminated. The main stem and the lower part of the lateral branches are all unnecessary. The only part of the plant you really need to grow is the tip of the growing terminal: the "cola bud," the very best part of the plant. This takes only a percentage of the time and effort it would take to grow a marijuana plant using the standard method.

We will take you through the whole process—step by step—from seed to clone to harvest. We will be describing a two-week cloning cycle, although options and alternatives will also be discussed. Follow the simple instructions, and soon you will begin your harvest—an endless supply of homegrown herb. Regardless of the size of your project, you will need some standard items, and you will have to follow some standard procedures. We used two different setups for demonstration purposes: one "greenhouse" system in a 50' long by 10' wide by 8' high trailer and a "closet system" in a small 4' by 4' room. Using these measurements you will be able to determine the approximate amount of marijuana a larger or smaller project will produce.

Although this book describes the process I call the "Sea of Green," it also utilizes the concept of the "perpetual harvest." This aspect of the book is one of its most important. Without it, the harvest would take place every eight to 12 weeks, and although you will have more flowers at the end of the 12-week period, you will grow more buds much faster by rotating the crops while they are in different stages of development. Since marijuana plants can replace cuttings every two weeks, it makes sense to rotate the crop every two weeks, and to organize your grow area to accommodate this rotation. In the author's [*and editor's*] opinion, this method of growing marijuana has become so standard that "Sea of Green" has come to imply "perpetual harvest" as a necessary part of it.

The *Sea of Green* book has been divided into two sections. The first section deals with general information concerning basic indoor cultivation directed at the marijuana grower, and the second section deals with my Sea of Green method specifically. As you progress through the second part of the book, the actual growing method, you may refer back to the general information to expand on all the major concepts.

The second section also details the exact process in a real-time scenario. This means that we take you from the germinating of the seed, step by step, showing you on a daily basis exactly what you need to do. Once you have been led through the entire process, you will be able to continue growing indefinitely. Following this repetitive structure, you will become knowledgeable, as it becomes more and more a learning process.

There is one thing that I would like to ask of you. That is, while you are in the process of growing your marijuana crop, you must endeavor to grow something else also. You must grow the truth about cannabis. Make sure that you do your part to see that it grows healthy and strong in the light of your consciousness. Then spread that light.

SECTION 1

GREENHOUSE SET-UP CROSS SECTION

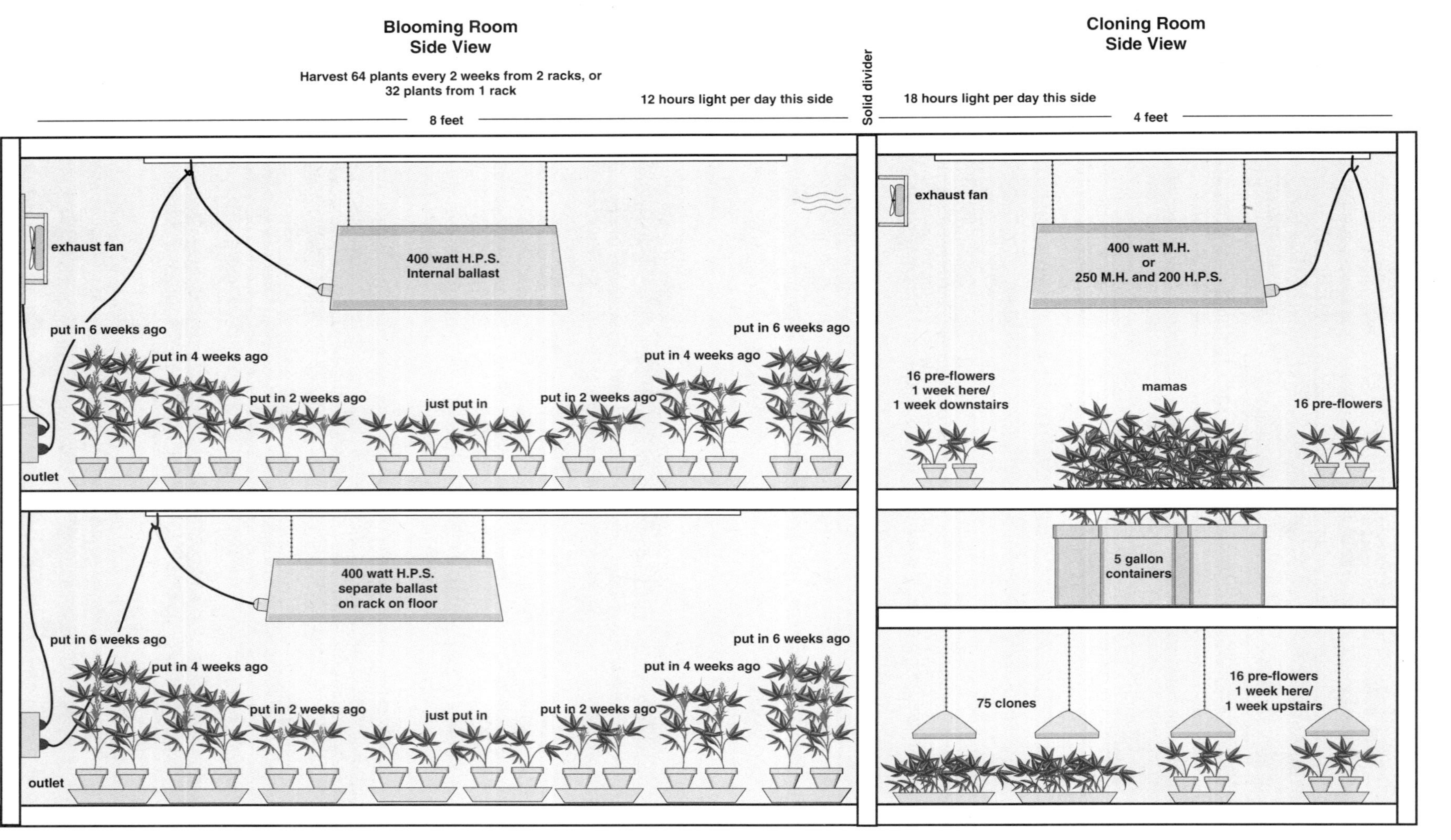

THE GROW ROOM

Before you start your crop, finding a good location and planning the layout of the space is essential. You will want to choose a place that only you have access to. If anyone else—neighbor, friend or passerby—can detect what is going on inside, the entire crop may be stolen. Even worse, your work could be discovered by law enforcement. Make sure that the rent is paid on time so that the landlord has no excuse to stop by and snoop. Don't play loud music or paint the outside of the structure in such a way as to draw attention to the area. Don't put Grateful Dead stickers or anti-Drug War stickers in the windows. And don't invite any friends—even your best friend or spouse—over to look at your system. This is how most grow rooms are busted.

You will also need to make sure the room has enough electrical power to run the lights, timers, exhaust system and other devices necessary for maintenance, and that it is large enough to contain all of the plants your mother plants (or as I like to call them, "mammas") will generate.

Most important, you should be comfortable with the location you choose. You will be spending a lot of time there.

Avoiding Detection

If you want to set up a greenhouse and cultivate large amounts, you probably won't want to do this project in your own home or on your own property. I have known people who rented out their own homes and moved to nice, secluded places in the country, so they could grow as much as they wanted. People have been known to dig up their backyard, build an underground bunker and cover it with a thin layer of soil, then put a patio set on top and an exhaust vent out the barbecue chimney. Another technique, popular in remote areas of the country where property values have dropped, is to set up shop on abandoned, secluded property. [*Editor's Note: However you decide to avoid detection by law enforcement, remember that if there is a property owner, he can be held liable for whatever you do on his property. And it's not good karma to involve unwitting participants in illegal activity.*]

For smaller, closet systems, avoiding detection is even easier. A growing area can be made from part of a garage with a simple fake wall. A large room may be partitioned with a secret passageway. A den can be built into a basement that would also conceal a secret growing area. A small, out-of-the-way room in any house can be concealed by building a wall over the entrance door to the room.

The secret is to be innovative. If you are using a small crawl space, like an attic, where you only have four feet in height to work with, you can grow your mammas in a horizontal position. This can be accomplished by simply tying down the growing tips and spacing them as they grow and lengthen. A 6' tall "mamma" can grow horizontally. With the proper spacing and pruning, the growth can be spread out more sideways and flattened, so the vertical growth is limited to the plant tips you want to clone.

Depending on which time of year you are planning to grow, temperature will be one of your major concerns. If it is very cold, you will want to make sure that your growing area is properly insulated in order to conserve as much energy as possible. If you must produce the heat, electric heaters are your safest bet. Their drawback is expense. If you use propane or kerosene as a heating source, you must be extremely careful. With the former, I suggest the use of a thermal coupling device to make sure that the propane will not turn on if the pilot light is not working. You can purchase standard propane heaters, used in houses, that have blowers built into them. If you are faced with a choice and you live in a cold climate, attics tend to be a little warmer (heat rises), while basements tend to be cooler.

If it is wintertime and you are using an outdoor area, such as an outbuilding, barn or storage room, you will find it difficult to get warm water to your crop. By placing a large, plastic garbage can in your room and using a fish aquarium heater, you will have all the hot water you need without leaving the room.

On the other hand, if you live in a warm climate, you will need some way to cool your area down. An air conditioner is suitable for this, although the expense can be formidable—especially in large growing areas.

Dividing the Area

The Sea Of Green method may be employed in almost any unused space. The selection of that space is up to you. Since there are certain standard requirements, we will cover them first, and see how they apply to the spot you have chosen for your project. You will need a space which you must be able to keep cool in the summer months and warm in the winter months, depending on when you are growing. You will want to choose a spot that is not in a position to be observed when you don't want it to be. This can sometimes be accomplished by simply keeping a lock on a closet or the door to a spare room.

Space is a major concern of all growers. Regardless of your project's size, it will be divided into two separate areas. We will refer to them as the cloning area and the blooming area. The cloning area, the smaller of the two spaces, is where we keep the mammas (the mother plants), the clones and the pre-flowering area. This is also where you will germinate your seeds. This area is on an 18-hour-a-day light cycle.

Setting Up a Greenhouse System

The size of the space required for the mammas is mathematically proportional to the amount of space you have available for your flowering plants in the blooming area. Here is how a large space could be divided up:

For the blooming area, I would recommend 36' long by 8' wide—288 square feet wide. Only one-sixth of this area would be used every two weeks, then there would be an 8' by 6' area for clones (48 square feet). It would take approximately 192 clones to fill that sized area; therefore you would want to make about 220 clones every two weeks. (I would end up using only the best 192 of the 220 clones.) Since it takes only about 11 or 12 properly pruned mother plants to produce 220 clones every two weeks, you would need a space for the mammas about 4' wide and 8' long. This size space will suffice for 11 or 12 mammas which would have the capability to produce 20 clones per plant—220 each and every two weeks.

Let's look at how big a space would be needed for cloning using these same figures. First determine what kind of container you will be using to clone into. For mathematical reference we will calculate using the largest size of the suggested clone containers: 3" wide peat-moss cups. These containers will be placed into 10 1/2" by 21" trays. That means that each tray will hold 32 clones at one time—your cloning area will have to hold 7 trays of 32 clones each, which will amount to 224 clones. An area of 4' by 4', or an area 2' by 8' will work perfectly. You will even have a little room left over to space your trays a bit.

The size area you needed for your pre-flowering space is the same size as the 1/6th area needed each two weeks in the blooming area. That is because the pre-flowering area will be holding the plants that will go into each 1/6th of the blooming area every two weeks. Therefore you will need an area 6' by 8' for the pre-flowering area.

DIAGRAM ON OPPOSITE PAGE:
THE SEA OF GREEN SYSTEM REQUIRES FOUR DIFFERENT AREAS FOR GROWING. THE FIRST AREA IS FOR MOTHER PLANTS. THE SECOND AREA HOLDS FRESH CUTTINGS (CLONES) FROM THE MOTHER PLANT, AND ANOTHER AREA IS SET UP FOR PREFLOWERS (CLONES THAT HAVE GROWN FOR A FEW WEEKS, BUT HAVE NOT DEVELOPED BUDS). THE LAST SECTION IS SET UP FOR THE CLONES TO MATURE INTO FLOWERING BUDS. ONCE THE CLONES MATURE, THEY ARE READY FOR HARVEST.

The Cloning Area

The area where you keep the mother plants, clones and pre-flowers I will refer to as the cloning area. Here, three distinct functions of your work will be performed. Their common bond is that they will all utilize light for 18 hours a day. This is why it is reasonable that they share the same room or area. (The blooming area where the flowering takes place requires light 12 hours a day, so it must be in a separate space.)

Each separate function in the cloning area will require a certain amount of space. We will demonstrate a few different structural arrangements of this area. We will also demonstrate a few different configurations of the blooming area because not everyone has the same-shaped space available to flower the plants in.

Regardless of the configuration of the cloning area or room, there are certain standard requirements. This is also true for the blooming area or room.

In the cloning room you will need space for your mammas. This area would be 8' by 4' in the greenhouse system. The cloning area would use a 400-watt metal halide on a 6' moving rail and its own timer, both of which need separate electrical outlets. This

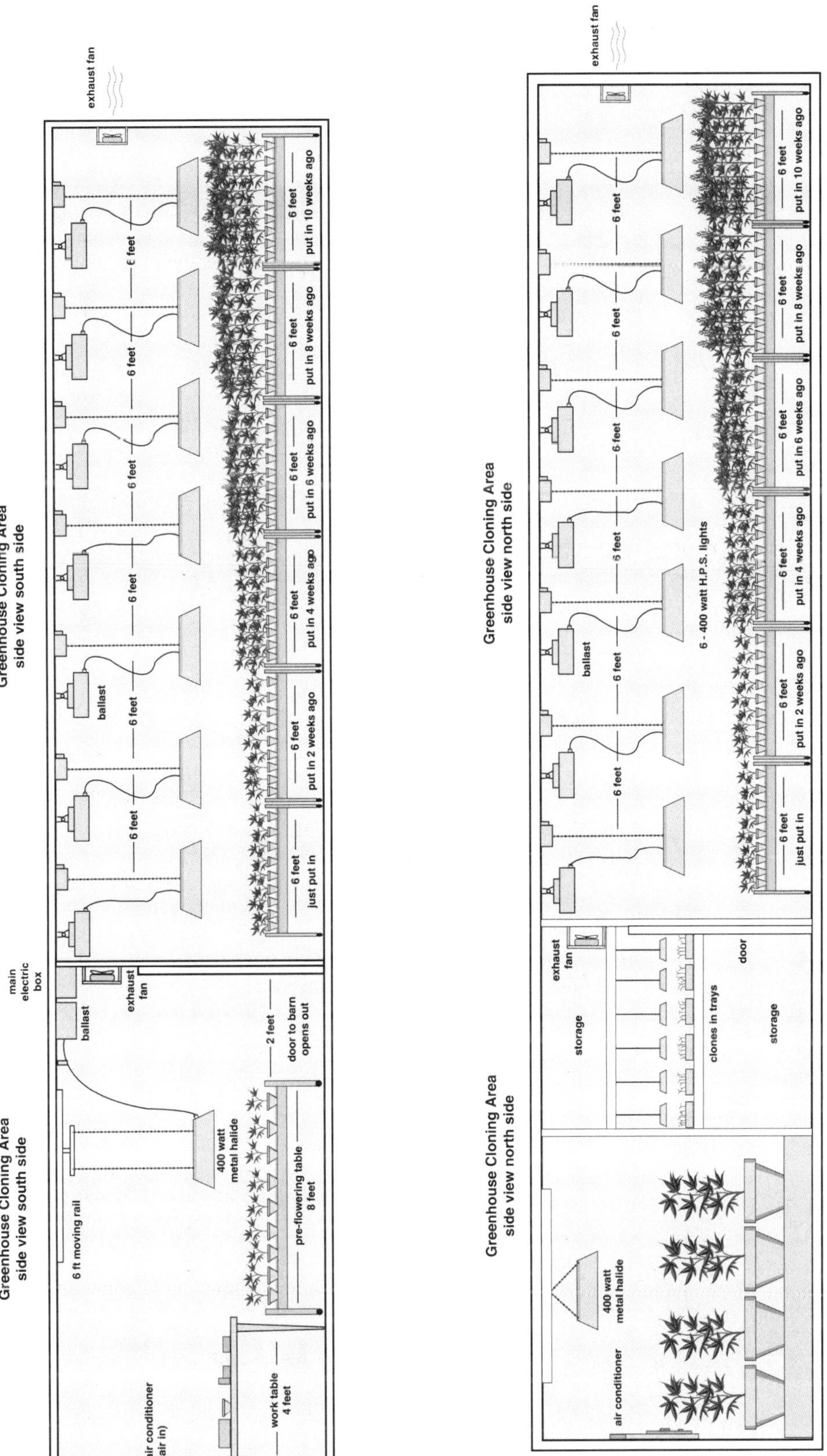

GREENHOUSE SET-UP CROSS SECTION

area will hold about a dozen mother plants. They are in 5-gallon containers (either peat moss or plastic).

Set up the containers so they are sitting on heavy-duty plastic, and the perimeter of the plastic on the floor should overlap a raised wooden edge, which will prevent any overflow of water from the mammas to out of the contained area. This can be done simply by placing a 2" by 2" wooden perimeter around the area for the mammas. Draping the plastic floor covering over the top of the wood, then placing the plants on top of the plastic, should keep the rest of the cloning area high and dry. I also keep a thermometer in this area. It is always a good idea to know what the temperature is at any given time.

The second part of your cloning area is where you will keep your clones. For the greenhouse setup, I suggest using 40-watt fluorescent grow bulbs as a light source. The fixtures are available in 4' or 8' lengths. Be sure that you hang them so that they may be lowered and raised. This is easily accomplished with the use of wire, cord, or chain and some simple screw-in hooks. The actual cloning rack or shelf should be covered with a layer of thick plastic, in case of spillage. A thermometer should also be kept in this area.

The third area in the cloning room is the pre-flowering area. This space is lit by its own 400-watt metal halide. The purpose of this area is to get the fastest growth possible from the plants during the two weeks they will be here. It also is connected to a 6' long moving rail that can allow the light to be raised or lowered, provided you attach it to a chain system. Metal halides come in smaller wattages if your pre-flowering area doesn't need this much light.

Setting Up a Closet System

A smaller space such as a closet, attic or basement can also be divided into two separate areas. We used a 4' wide X 4' deep X 8' high closet to create our closet grow area. Like bunk beds, one area was placed on top of the other. A solid divider separated the two to facilitate the two different light requirements. Either the blooming are or the cloning area could be on top. (See diagram on opposite page).

The cloning area was lit with a 400-watt metal halide. It contained the two mammas which take up a space that measured about 2' wide X 4' deep X 4' high . It also contained one 10 1/2" X 21" tray that held approximately 32 clones, and two more trays with approximately 16 to 20 preflowers.

The blooming area (also 4' X 4') was divided into four separate areas because the variety we used had an 8-week blooming cycle. Each two weeks we would fill up 1/4 of the blooming area, which would hold 16 to 20 plants in 5 1/4" containers. The blooming area was lit with a 400-watt high-pressure sodium lamp. Exhaust fans and oscillating fans will help create a cool and even flow of air in the small area.

In this kind of setup you would take 32 clones every two weeks, keep the best 16 to 20 of these and turn them into pre-flowers every two weeks. Then 16 to 20 pre-flowers would be placed in the blooming area every two weeks, and 16 to 20 would be harvested every two weeks.

CUTTINGS FROM THE MOTHER PLANT ARE TRANSPLANTED INTO SMALL, 5 1/2" SQUARE CONTAINERS. USING PLASTIC TRAYS (SIZED 10 1/2" X 21") TO KEEP 8 SQUARE CONTAINERS TOGETHER WILL HELP KEEP THE GROWING AREAS ORGANIZED AND EFFICIENTLY MAINTAINED.

Air Circulation

One problem with indoor growing is that lights can overheat a grow room—even a small closet setup. An oscillating fan, attached to the roof or a nearby window, will help keep the room at an even temperature. It will circulate the cooler air from outdoors with the warmer interior air. Installing it at the top of the ceiling will also cool the warmer air, because it tends to rise. This air circulatrion also has a drying effect and keeps the humidity down. A musty, fungal smell in your grow room is an indicator that you do not have adequate ventilation. If your humidity is higher than you can control, you should consider the use of a dehumidifier. These are available at most large hardware and department stores.

The cloning area will require an exhaust fan system. Exhaust fans

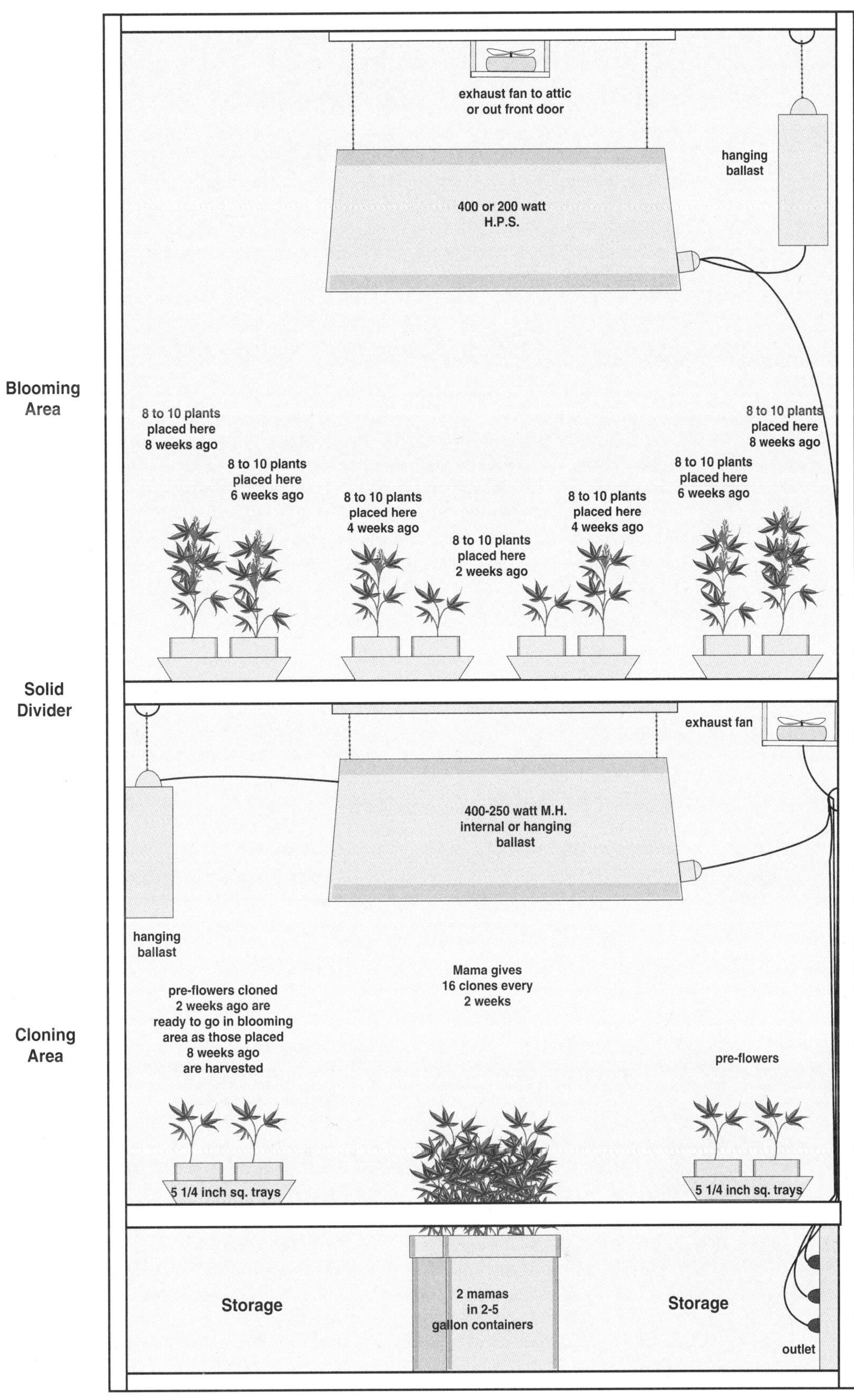

CLOSET SET-UP CROSS SECTION

come in a variety of sizes, and their power is measured by cfm rating (cubic feet per minute). The cfm is determined by multiplying the dimensions of the room it is to be used in. A room 50' by 10' wide and 8' high would be 4000 cubic feet. A fan with a 2270 cfm rating would take approximately two minutes to exhaust the air from the room. (I think it's important to use a fan that can exhaust a room in two or three minutes.)

For the greenhouse setup, a large attic fan of approximately 2270 cfm. was used in both growing areas (see diagrams for details). It also employed a small exhaust fan (approximately 150 cfm), often used for bathrooms, to exhaust from the cloning area to the blooming area.

For a closet growing area, I use the same small "bathroom" exhaust fans. Another popular fan is known as the "squirrel cage.

You may consider setting up your exhaust system in two ways: exhaust each room separately (blowing the air out of each room to the exterior), or exhaust air from the cloning area into the blooming area (or vice versa, blowing the air out of one room area and into another, then outdoors). Since excessive heat is most often the problem when growing indoors, and heat rises, the exhaust fan should be near the top of your cloning or blooming area.

As you can see in the *Sea Of Green* videotape, I used a small piece of metal tubing to connect the cloning area and the blooming area. This prevents light from the cloning area from leaking into the blooming room. (I bend the metal tubing so that no light can pass through.) A manual control of the fan will assist in regulating the temperature of the cloning room. I also like to use thermostats and variable speeds on my exhaust systems. This gives me the ability to control the exhaust speeds, and to circulate air when a certain room temperature is reached. By connecting a timer to the exhaust system, you can circulate the air when you're not in the room. (This is especially useful in grow room setups that require a minimum of visits.)

Smaller grow areas can heat up even more quickly than larger setups. If this happens in any area, you should put an exhaust fan there. This is a common problem with small or walk-in closets.

Make sure that the exhaust system is camouflaged. A curious neighbor or passerby can cause big problems otherwise. Both the exhaust and entrance portals should also be screened properly to keep insects from entering.

For large grow rooms, we use either rolls of thick, black polyurethane plastic, or 4' by 8' Styrofoam sheets to make dividers for the separate areas, if the project is done in one room. First, I take outdoor-treated 2" by 2" (or 2" by 4") lumber, then paint any exposed surfaces with flat-white, outdoor, enamel paint. Then I construct the dividers and partition off the areas, according to the floor plan I devise for the space.

If you are doing your own wiring, be sure to have the proper circuit breakers, and make sure everything is up to code. Your 1000-watt ballast and bulb will obviously require a stronger-gauge wire to run electricity through than a 40-watt fluorescent.

Be careful not to overload your circuits. You never want to take shortcuts with electricity as it can kill you in a second. If you are not completely qualified to do your own wiring, I suggest you purchase a good *Wiring Simplified* book. If you are still not sure, find someone who is, even if that means hiring a professional.

IF THE GROWING AREA IS TOO SMALL TO HOLD ALL OF THE PLANTS, BUILDING TABLES FOR HOLDING CLONES IS A GOOD WAY TO CREATE MORE SPACE. PUTTING A RACK ON TOP OF THE TABLE FOR FLUORESCENT LIGHT FIXTURES WILL ALSO ENABLE YOU TO ENSURE THAT THE PLANTS GET ALL THE LIGHT THEY NEED. THE RACKS ON THIS TABLE WERE MADE WITH 2" X 2" BOARDS, WHICH ALLOWS FOR BETTER AIR FLOW AROUND THE PLANTS.

Dividing the Grow Areas for Lighting Efficiency

If you have a large blooming area, you will want to maximize your lighting potential. In the *Sea of Green* videotape, we ran the 400-watt high-pressure sodium over the 10' by 36' area. In order to obtain maximum use of the light, we divided the blooming space into two separate areas. One area was 4' wide and 36' long, in which the plant tables were nailed to the wall. The tables for the other 4' by 36' area were placed on rollers, so they could be easily moved. When these roller-tables were placed on the opposite wall of the room, it created a 2' aisle down the center. This made it possible to walk down the center and tend to all the plants at the same time. When standing in the center of the room, the most distant plant will be four feet away.

When the plants are not being tended to, the roller-tables can be moved to a place adjacent to those nailed to the wall. This creates a 36' long by 8' wide blooming area. This area may be easily covered with a light on a 6 ft. long moving rail. One end of the rail is placed one foot from the wall and covers the entire distance across the width of the plants (8 feet), extending to exactly one foot from the other end.

The walls of the blooming area should be wrapped with 2' high reflecting material. With the light coming to within one foot of the end of the 8' wide area, and the reflective material supplementing the end sections with even more light, the plants situated at the end sections will receive sufficient light.

Lengthwise, I placed the lights 6' apart. This way, the rays from each separate light overlap at 3' from the center of each light. This means that each plant receives light from all sides.

For a smaller setup, like the closet area described above, you can run the entire system with two 400-watt bulbs: a metal halide for the mammas, clones and preflowers, and a high pressure sodium (HPS) for the blooming plants. The cloning area can be placed on the bottom, and the blooming area on top.

When building roller-tables or shelves for holding plant trays, I always find it useful to angle or slant them so that if the trays are overwatered, the excess water will fall to the front of the table. This will help insure that the soil will hold only as much water as needed.

PICTURED ABOVE IS A CLOSET SYSTEM WHERE THE CLONING AREA HOUSES TWO MAMMAS (AT RIGHT), TWO TRAYS OF PRE-FLOWERS (REAR OF PHOTO), AND ONE TRAY (10 1/2" X 21") WITH 32 CLONES IN 2 1/4" PEAT MOSS SQUARES (FRONT OF PHOTO).

Equipment and Materials

Below is a list of all the materials you will need to purchase once you have decided on the layout of your grow room. Although I have suggested where to buy them, a search in the Yellow Pages or on the Internet might find a better price. Also, although an indoor grow room can be set up at any time and in any part of the world, remember that some nurseries and garden stores are open seasonally. If you decide to start growing in the dead of winter, it might be difficult to find the supplies you need.

We have included a chart to help you calculate equipment costs.

1. I suggest all construction of wall frames be done with 2" by 2" or 2" by 4" boards, depending on the strength required of your particular construction. For walls I suggest either thick black polyurethane plastic, or Styrofoam sheets (no need for sheetrock). For the bottom of tables or racks, I suggest 1/4" plywood, or 2" by 2" boards placed a few inches apart. Always use outdoor-treated wood whenever you can. Plastic or non-rusting metal is also suitable for your frames.

These materials are available at lumberyards or hardware stores.

2. For a small grow room, you will need a watering device, such as a standard watering can. This may also be used to administer fertilizer, lime, B1, etc. (but obviously not pesticides). For larger projects, a rubber hose connected to a water tap will come in handy. A separate device will be needed to administer insecticides or fungicides, if necessary, as well as a second hand-pump spray for watering and washing plants. A turkey baster can be used to remove excess water, but a sponge or dry rag can be used for small setups or by the budget-conscious.

The local nursery, department store and/or garden store stocks most of these.

3. Your decision on how large or small you want your project to be determines how many metal-halide, high-pressure sodium and fluorescent lights you will need. You will use metal-halide on the mammas and the pre-flowering area, the cloning space will use fluorescent grow lights and the blooming area will use high-pressure sodium.

These are available through specialty stores, certain mail-order outlets, and indoor garden stores. (Remember never to mention marijuana or illegal activity in these stores.)

4. You will need exhaust fans or blowers and standard window screening for each ventilation exit or entrance. Again, the size and quantity will depend upon the size of your project. They will need thermostat controls and variable-speed controls. You will require thermometers in both the cloning area and the blooming area. A negative air ionizer ($100-150), which will eliminate the odor from the plants, is strongly recommended, especially if you are growing in a populated area.

Other devices that you might want to purchase include a heating unit (electrical heater or a propane setup), an air conditioner, and a dehumidifier.

These can be purchased at any hardware store. Very large department stores with a good housewares department will sometimes offer a considerable selection.

5. You will need a full-spectrum vegetative fertilizer and a full-spectrum blooming fertilizer. You will also want the transplanting aid and root stimulant B1. SuperThrive is suggested also.

These can be purchased at nurseries and garden stores. Large department stores with a garden center sometimes stock them.

6. For the standard soil mixture you will need a good potting soil, coarse horticultural perlite, hydrated lime and pasteurized cow manure. You will also require a container to mix your soil in.

These can be purchased at nurseries and garden stores, and many flower shops. Large department stores with a garden center sometimes stock them.

7. For the germinating process you will need containers—small peat moss cups, plastic cups or root cubes to germinate your seeds. You will also require 10 1/2" by 21" plastic trays for storing the seedling and cloning containers. You will need 5 1/4" squares to transplant your seedlings and clones into. The mammas need large containers—5-gallon to 7-gallon.

These can be found at most nurseries and garden stores. Large department stores or garden centers also stock them.

THE STANDARD SOIL MIX REQUIRES GOOD POTTING SOIL, COARSE HORTICULTURAL PERLITE, HYDRATED LIME, AND PASTEURIZED COW MANURE. (WORM CASTINGS OR OTHER ORGANIC ADDITIVES CAN BE USED IN PLACE OF MANURE.) ALWAYS BE SURE TO PURCHASE ALL OF THE ITEMS YOU WILL NEED BEFORE YOU START YOUR PROJECT.

8. You will also need a sharp blade and an antifungal cloning liquid, powder or gel and some small stickers. Again, your best bet is a nursery or garden supply store.

9. Three very helpful tools are a pH indicator with a long probe, a light indicator, and a very strong magnifying glass. Except for the magnifying glass, which can be found at most department stores, you will find these items at a nursery or garden supply store.

If you want to prepare for a possible bug infestation, the purchase of diatomaceous earth and organic pyrethrums (available as liquids, powders or bombs) is recommended. You should decide for yourself, based on your budget, whether you want to spend the money on these items now, or wait until you are faced with a bug problem. Once the bugs arrive and you decide that the use of insecticides is called for, purchase rubber gloves, an apron, and a second sprayer. (If the bug infestation gets serious, you will need a container large enough to hold the entire plant.) Some of the common brand names are Ortho, Chacon and Attack, although there are many other manufacturers of pyrethrum-based insecticides. The insecticides are available at most nurseries, garden stores, or garden departments in large department stores.

You might consider purchasing predator mites at some point, but they are not something you can buy and keep on hand. If you don't provide bugs for them to eat, they will starve to death. However, once you decide to try them, 1500 ladybugs will cost only $5-10 at a local nursery. Other prices are available through the mail-order suppliers I recommend in the chapter on pests,

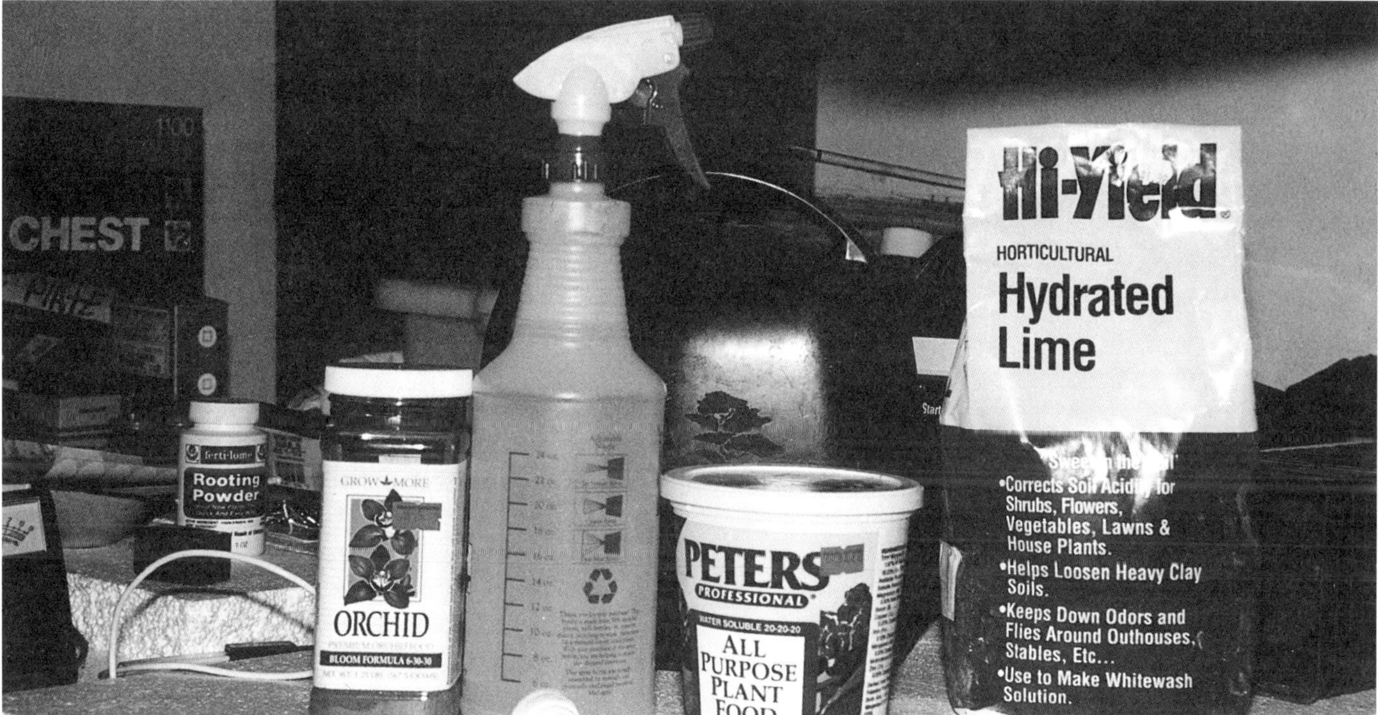

SOME ITEMS ARE SEASONAL, SO YOU MIGHT HAVE TO STOCK UP, ESPECIALLY DURING THE WINTER MONTHS. GROWING INDOORS CAN BE DONE AT ANY TIME OF THE YEAR AND THROUGHOUT THE YEAR.

but I do not recommend buying anything through the mail for security reasons.

10. Sheets of thick (4 millimeter to 6 millimeter), clear or black plastic will be needed for dividing the rooms into areas. It's usually available in rolls of 50-100 feet. A reflective material, such as Mylar, will also be necessary. Most hardware stores keep this in stock.

11. Be sure to make a visit to the local hardware store for a hammer (standard size), saw, drill, staple gun, nails (large enough for 2" by 2" and 2" by 4" pieces of wood), hooks, and chains. I usually use a drill when bolting a unit together (if nails aren't strong enough), or to start holes for nails that I think might break the board I'm nailing into, but it's also good for making the process more accurate. (A starter hole for a nail should be 1/2 the circumference of the nail). Use longer staples when attaching softer material (sheets of clear/black plastic or Mylar), and shorter staples for harder materials (cardboard, wire, plywood, etc.). Usually 1/4" to 1/2" staples fit the bill for most materials.

Additional hardware that might come in handy: hinges and screws (for large grow rooms, in case you need to add a door); chains or cords with eyelets (to hang lights); duct tape (useful for taping black plastic over windows—to keep unnecessary light out); a fire extinguisher and a smoke alarm (important safety considerations). If you're thinking about the long-term investment you're making in the grow room setup, you might consider bolting all construction elements so that the partitions are portable and can be moved to a future location.

12. Moving tracks for lights are recommended for anyone attempting a large, sophisticated setup. They're available at most specialty stores that carry hydroponic equipment, and most stores that have HID lights. The moving rails cost about $150 apiece. There is an additional device that causes the light fixture to stall at each end for a minute. These "stall" systems cost about $25 apiece, but are well worth the investment. I screw them into the ceiling or onto the side of a 2" by 4" eight-footer (board), and then secure it to the racks or the ceiling. The light movers each have a capacity of 25 lbs.

Some light movers are designed to move in a circle, but I never bother with them.

13. Important: Don't forget rolling papers or your favorite pipe, and matches or a lighter.

LIGHTING

Getting enough light to your plants is a very important part of the process. You can have the best seeds, the right soil mix, and follow all the directions to the letter, but if you try to cut corners by using less light than your plants need, it will all go to waste. The only way your plants will develop full, flowering buds is if their need for proper lighting is met.

Photoperiod

The photoperiod is the relationship between the number of hours of daylight and the number of hours of darkness in any given 24-hour period. Marijuana, like most plants, is photoperiodic. This means that the primary environmental factor which determines when marijuana will begin to flower is the light period. The amount of daily light a plant *doesn't* get will determine this. Marijuana is what we refer to as a short-day, or long-night, bloomer.

We will be manipulating this light period to our advantage in two different ways: once for determining the gender of our parent seedlings, and again to make our clones flower for harvest.

When a marijuana plant has grown from the initial seed planting stage after about two months, you can manipulate the light period and force the plant to flower. If a plant is given 18 hours of constant light each day it will continue to grow in the vegetative state. The plant will grow as if it were always June 22, the day of the year with the longest amount of daylight. If you take that same plant and start it on a cycle of 12 hours of uninterrupted darkness and 12 hours of light, the plant will enter the flowering stage after approximately two weeks.

High-Pressure Sodium (HPS)

For the best flowering potential, I suggest the use of high-pressure sodium light, placed as close to your plants as possible without burning them, for the 12-hour light cycle. I suggest starting the high-pressure sodium light 12 inches from the tops of the plants. If you decide to use a moving rail with your light fixtures, set them to lower the HPS light to as close as 6 inches to the plants.

Be careful if adjusting the lights any lower than 12 inches. If your buds begin to stretch and "run" in an abnormal fashion, your light is too close. The same is true when using any wattage of light. Start the lights at the recommended distance to the plant, then over a period of time lower the lights until they are as close to the plants as possible without burning them. The combination of the reduced light period and the intense HPS will give your plants the proper conditions for flowering.

The only place the high-pressure sodium light is needed is in the blooming area. This is because the HPS gives the best spectrum of light needed for the plants to flower, while the metal halide, discussed below, gives the best light for the other stages of plant growth. The HPS will only be turned on for 12 hours a day. This is done to induce flowering by the manipulation of the photoperiod. Once the plants start receiving the lesser amount of light it triggers the hormones which stop the vegetative growth. The HPS produces more light on the red end of the light spectrum. It is this red light that affects the flowering hormones and thus produces flowers (a.k.a. buds).

The HPS should be kept the same distance from the tops of the plants as was the light in the pre-flowering area, which is where they were before going to the blooming area. I suggest 6" to 12". If you require more than two 400-watt lights you may want to consider the use of a 1000-watt. If I use more than one HPS, I sometimes position them side by side in a row 6' apart.

HPS lights come in a variety of sizes. This gives you a much larger range of sizes for your flowering area. They come in wattages of 35, 50, 100, 200, 400, 1000 and some in between. You do not want to use low-pressure sodium lights.

Fluorescents

I strongly suggest using fluorescent lights for seedlings and clones, as well as when determining the gender. The standard 4', two-bulb shop-light fixtures will work best for most grow rooms, although fluorescents are also available in lengths of 5, 6, 7 and 8 feet or longer. (Shorter fluorescent bulbs are not recommended, as they do not provide enough light for the plants.) Sylvania's Standard Gro-Lux tubes or Westinghouse Agro-Lite tubes are both sufficient for use with the fixtures.

The 4' long, two-bulb, 40-watt fluorescent lights adequately cover an area the same as their own length—four feet long—but the width of their coverage is only 1 foot (six inches from the center of the fixture on either side). Therefore, if you require the use of more than one fluorescent light, you should place each fixture a foot apart. Since the clones are in the same close proximity to the mammas and the pre-flowering area, they will receive supplemental metal halide light from them. If you would like to use V.H.O. fluorescent lights, be sure to use a fixture ballast suited especially for V.H.O. fluorescent. They use more electricity, but will increase your light.

Metal Halide (MH)

I insist upon using metal halide lights in the cloning area, for the seedlings, for the mammas and for the pre-flowering area. These metal halides (and HPS), are also called high intensity discharge (HID) lights. They need to be handled carefully. Your metal halide should have a tempered safety glass to protect it from accidental damage, or to prevent even one drop of water from hitting it—this will cause it to explode. It is a good idea to place your metal halide ballast on a small stand if it is going to sit on the floor. This is because a water spill on the floor could have some shocking results. A simple stand is two 1' long, 2" by 4" boards with a 1/2" by 1' long, 6" wide plank sitting on top of the 2" by 4"s. I prefer to hang the ballast from the roof with heavy-duty chains and hooks. Another method of keeping them out of the way is to fasten them securely to the walls. The ballast should have its own electrical socket, and its own timer. If you use a metal halide ballast, use a metal halide bulb. Also, be sure your system includes the proper reflector.

Metal halide lamps come in a variety of wattages, including 175, 250, 400, 1000 and 1500. I prefer the Super Metal Halide, as it only costs a few more dollars, but gives almost 25% more lumens. I also suggest use of the "clear light" bulb.

Safety Tips

Here are some simple safety tips for HID lights: You should never look directly into any lit metal halide or high-pressure sodium bulb. You should also never try to remove a bulb from a fixture while it is hot. In fact, you should avoid moving the fixture at all after it has been turned on for any length of time. Always move lamps when they have been turned off for a while and the bulbs are cool.

If you decide to install your lights on a moving rail, make sure that the cords will not get tangled in anything when the fixture is moving on the rail.

Whenever your HID light is turned off, whether on purpose or accidentally, always wait at least fifteen minutes before turning it back on. Turning it on before then will stress the system.

Do not place your bulb at an irregular angle. It is specifically designed to be used either vertically or horizontally.

Never use a HPS bulb, ballast or fixture with a metal halide. The parts are not interchangeable and doing so can be dangerous.

It has been reported that infrared devices used by law enforcement agencies to detect grow rooms can easily spot light devices that use 1000-watt bulbs (or higher). This is especially true when attics or other rooms close to a roof are used for growing. This is another reason to use the 400-watt bulbs, even if cultivating large amounts.

METAL HALIDE LIGHTS ARE USED FOR GIVING MOTHER PLANTS AND VEGETATIVE PLANTS 18 HOURS OF LIGHT PER DAY.

Feeding Plants Light

I have found that a 400-watt metal halide will suitably cover an area 6' wide and 6' to 10' long, if placed on a 6' to 8' moving rail and kept on for 18 hours a day. If the 400-watt is stationary, 6' by 4' is about the limit of good coverage. (Good growth requires a minimum of 20 watts per square foot, and 30 is often recommended).

Once your seedlings have germinated and grown for about four weeks, you will want to place them under a metal halide and increase their light diet. I like to start with a 400-watt metal halide placed about 24" from the tops of the new seedlings. As they become accustomed to the stronger light the lamp should be slowly lowered. If it is on a moving rail, I try to get the light fixture situated anywhere from 6" to 12" from the tops of the plants. If the light is stationary, I keep the fixture anywhere from 12-18" from the tops of the plants. I do not suggest using any light over 400 watts for the seedlings, or more than 18 hours daily.

If you use a smaller than 400-watt metal halide, you will be able to move the light fixture closer to the seedlings. Use your common sense here and start your light a little farther away from the seedlings, working your way closer. I usually use the metal halide kept in the area for the mammas to light the seedlings. This is because once the gender of the seedlings is determined, the remaining female seedlings will always become mother plants.

Once the seedlings are sexed, you will throw all your males away. You will then keep the best of the females and they will become the new mammas. You simply keep the metal halide on them as they are cloned each two weeks. The light is kept on 18 hours daily throughout the mother plant's lifetime.

As you clone your mother plants every two weeks, the clones from the previous two weeks will become your pre-flowers. This is the other place you will need a metal halide. The plants pictured in this book will all be in 5 1/4" square containers. In large systems, the use of a moving track for the metal halide lamp and constructive positioning of the mammas and pre-flowers will require only one light fixture for both areas. Remember they are both on an 18-hour-a-day light schedule. You should turn the metal halide on and off once a day if possible.

IF YOUR GROWING AREA NEEDS TO USE MORE THAN ONE FLUORESCENT LIGHT, THEN EACH FIXTURE SHOULD BE PLACED ONE FOOT APART, AS SHOWN ABOVE.

Electricity

I am not going to attempt to give a class on electricity. Whether you are called upon to do the entire wiring for your project, or just some simple job, be careful and know what you are doing. It is my suggestion that you purchase a *Wiring Simplified* manual or have someone knowledgeable help you, even if this means hiring a professional. Another alternative for the electrically illiterate is to buy pre-wired hardware from a grow store.

I will discuss a few safety tips. After all, any time you put electricity and water together in the same room there is danger, because water conducts electricity. If you are careless, or allow a careless person in your grow room, there is the danger that someone will be electrocuted.

Do not ever touch anything you think might be hot with the inside of your hand. If you must touch something you are not sure of, make a fist and touch it with the back of your hand or your knuckle. This way if something is alive or hot, your hand will not tighten on the item. If you grab something and it is alive, you may not be able to let go.

Use only one hand when working with any electrical equipment—the most dangerous situation is when electricity passes through two sources, and a person becomes the conductor.

Before you plug in a metal halide or a high-pressure sodium light, make sure that the attached fuse and circuit breaker are the proper size. I never put two of these on one wall outlet. Be sure anything you plug in has the proper fuse and breaker. Never overload an outlet. Make sure that any wire you use is the proper gauge.

Use a ground for all electrical devices in the room. Check carefully to make sure that what you tap into is really a ground. Follow the wire you think is grounded, making sure there are no breaks in between.

I have found that a 5000-watt Honda generator is an excellent alternative for backup power, or may even be used as your main power source. You can run six 400-watt HIDs, a dozen fluorescents, some fans and even an air-conditioner on just one of these. (You can even add a radio.) With constructive placement, a generator can be muffled quite well. Digging it into the ground is one way. Placing it in a small, well-insulated building with adequate ventilation is another. Remember, carbon monoxide must be evacuated out of any enclosed area containing a generator before you enter that area.

Calculating Electrical Costs

Figuring out how much the electrical system for a grow room will cost is a simple matter, and since a sudden surge in electrical use can indicate that a person is growing marijuana, it is something you should plan ahead of time.

Electrical costs for most parts of the country cost, on the average, 3-8 cents per kilowatt (KW) hour. Let's say you are being charged five cents per KW hour. A garden that uses only two 400-watt metal halide lights 18 hours per day (plus an exhaust fan and a light mover) would draw approximately 1,000 to 1,200 watts per month (approximately $70 per month). Add in any other electrical costs (fluorescent lights, heater or air conditioner, dehumidifier, etc.) and even a relatively small arrangement not only ends up costing a significant amount of money, but can also alert the utility company that something unusual is going on.

If possible, defray the extra costs by using external and independent energy sources (solar energy, diesel generator, propane heater, etc.). We have also provided a chart to assist you in calculating these electrical costs. Of course, you should also check your electrical system to insure that it can handle the extra load from the additional electrical devices.

YOUR BIGGEST ELECTRICAL EXPENSES WILL BE FOR THE LIGHT SYSTEM. DEPENDING UPON THE LOCAL CLIMATE AND THE TIME OF YEAR, ELECTRICAL COSTS SHOULD ALSO BE TAKEN INTO CONSIDERATION FOR HEATING AND/OR COOLING THE GROWING AREAS.

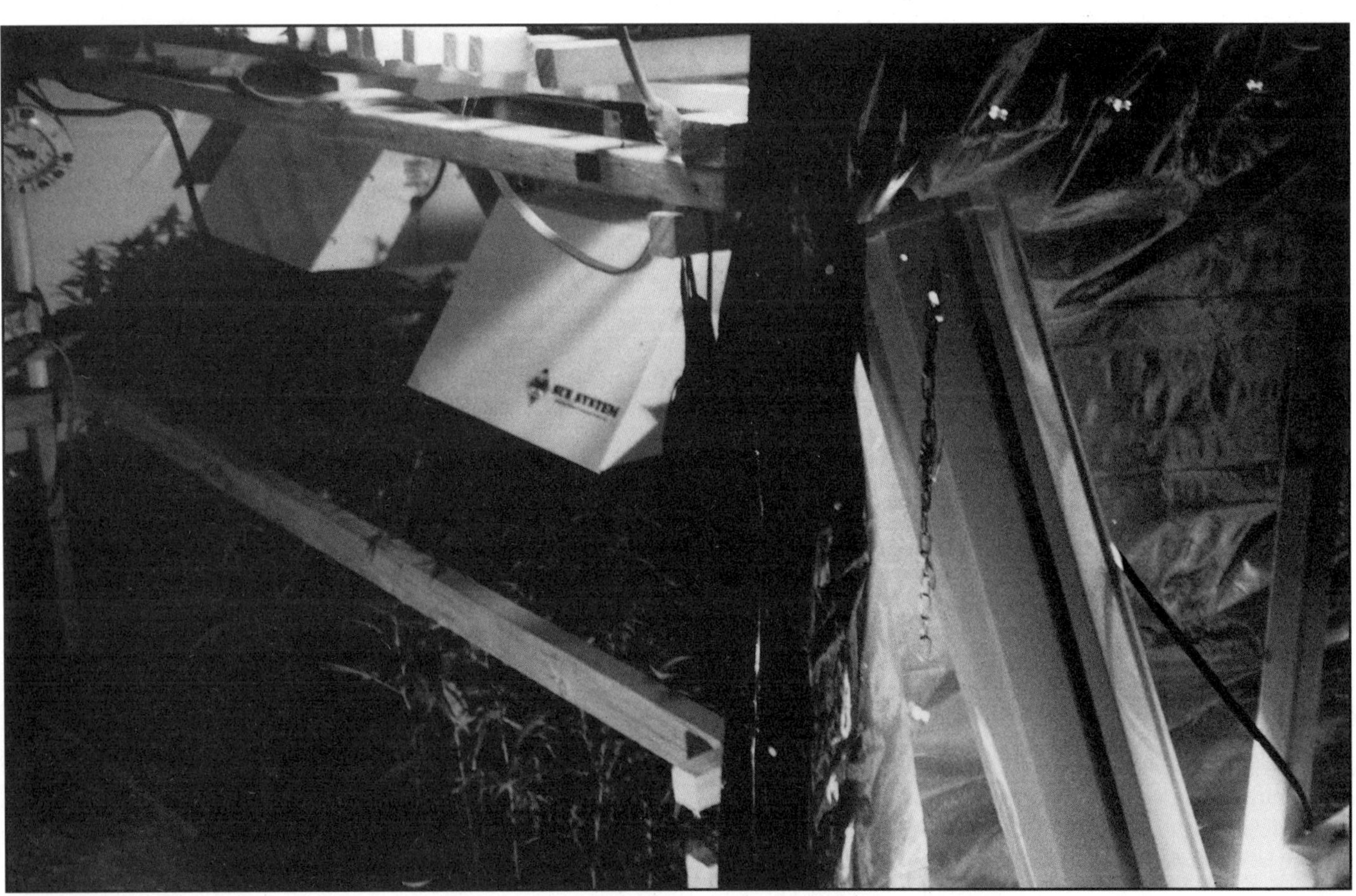

Fifteen Tips
for Keeping the Grow Room Cool and Safe

1. Odor control: Incorporate negative-ion generators, time-dispensed aerosol fragrance and scores of plug-in style air fresheners.

2. Aside from snitches, infrared detectors and electrical bills are two of the most common ways by which growing operations are detected by law enforcement. Heat buildup problems can usually be handled by leaving the exhaust fan running while the lights are on.

3. Air conditioners use a lot of electricity. Drawing air from the coolest room in the house (i.e. the basement) will help keep the room cooler.

4. Swamp coolers (evaporative coolers) can be used in dry climates. These devices cool air by circulating water over cedar pads, and add water to the air.

5. Cooling the light fixtures with a small fan can remove the need to rely on an air conditioner. Building a glass partition below the lights and above the plants will create two climates in the room, and make it even easier to keep the lights cool.

6. The best place to install the exhaust system is at the ceiling. An existing or new roof-level chimney provides a very efficient outlet for odors. If a chimney is impractical then crawl spaces, attics, casement windows, under stairs or even garages, or other rooms can be substituted.

7. Light is absorbed by dark objects, such as soil. Covering soil with white plastic will reflect the light up to the plants, and increase the amount of light that plants receive.

8. Using reflectors, or painting the walls of the grow room white, will increase the amount of light to the plants. Putting a white sheet of plastic on the floor will also help.

9. It's a good idea to wear UV-screening sunglasses when working in a grow room—especially when working with metal halide or high-pressure sodium light. Most sunglasses will do the job.

10. Clean the light fixtures when they have collected any dust, dirt or grime, which will cut down on the amount of light that they deliver. When changing bulbs, always turn the light off and wait unti they are at room temperature before changing.

11. If an HID light cracks or breaks, do not look at it. Look away and pull the plug. Again, wait for the bulb to cool before removing it.

12. Be sure that all electrical equipment is grounded. (Three-prong adaptor plugs are recommended for all devices.)

13. Never touch a light fixture or reflector when watering plants, or when the electricity is on.

14. Keep all electrical cords raised off the floor and away from water.

15. Never touch any metal object, such as a light reflector, when standing on a wet floor.

GROWING MEDIUMS

Containers

I will be describing standard containers throughout the process. I encourage anyone to use alternative methods and items if necessary. If you cannot get one of the containers mentioned below, see if you can come up with some suitable alternative. We have attempted to describe items that are available at any gardening supply center.

Each section of the room is a container in a sense, because we put a raised trim around each area, then lay thick plastic to line the bottom. This helps give 100% control over any water that may drip out the bottom of a container or any accidental over-watering or spillage.

I suggest purchasing trays of small plastic cups, larger 2 1/4" plastic cups, 2 1/4" peat moss cups and 5 1/4" square containers. We use these plastic trays for a variety of purposes. We like to keep the mammas in 2 or 5-gallon peat moss, clay or plastic pots.

Fill the small trays of plastic cups with the standard soil mixture and use them for germinating seeds and for cloning. The trays of small plastic cups fit perfectly into the plastic trays. The small individual plastic cups and the small peat moss cups are placed into the trays, which are then filled with one inch of water and used in the same fashion for cloning.

If you can't find the 5 1/4" plastic squares or want to save some money, use the bottom half of a clean, half-gallon milk carton. You can use small food cans in place of the smaller containers. A baking pan may become a tray or you can simply make a perimeter tray with the use of plastic draped over 2" by 2" boards, laid in a rectangle or square.

I have found that it is best not to recycle your containers once they have been used. The only containers I would reuse are the 5 1/4" squares, but only if the crop was clean and free of any problems, and then I would reuse them only one time. After that they usually become too brittle to use.

Soil

I always use a standard soil mixture or felt-type rooting cubes as the two mediums for all the stages of growth. However, if you prefer a soilless medium such as Rockwool, vermiculite, sand or gravel, or any other medium, feel free to use it. The Sea of Green process will be the same.

THE STANDARD SOIL MIXTURE I USE IS:

1. 1/2 part clean, commercial potting soil (I prefer Peter's)
2. 1/2 part coarse horticultural perlite
3. 1/24 part pasteurized cow manure (or worm castings or other organic additive)
4. Two heaping tablespoons horticultural hydrated lime

Add a little water to this mixture until your soil is of such a consistency that when you squeeze a handful into a ball it will stay in that shape, but when you squeeze the ball with your fingers it readily crumbles back into its original form.

Peter's, my suggested brand of soil, usually has a pH close to neutral. Perlite is an intensely heated sand, or volcanic glass. The heating process enlarges and expands the perlite, giving it an air-pocketed interior and an irregular pocketed surface. This gives it all the properties we require. The perlite will help the mixture to breathe and have better drainage. Perlite helps to keep the soil loose and aerated thus giving the roots ample room to grow properly. It usually has a pH close to neutral. The hydrated lime is fast-acting, the purpose of which is to help neutralize and assure the proper pH from the start, whenever you use the soil mixture. Be sure to use horticultural lime—never use quicklime. The organic, pasteurized worm castings add nutrients and texture to your soil.

Whenever you mix the soil be sure to wear proper breathing apparatus. If you are mixing it indoors you should have a fan blowing the exhaust out an open window. It is not healthy to breathe Perlite, nor dust from the other items.

You will find this standard soil mixture to be of a loamy nature—unlike regular soil, dirt or clay. It will be loose and aerated, which allows the root systems of the plants to easily penetrate the soil. Loose soil also insures proper water drainage. Your soil will be able to breathe, which enables aerobic microbes to live and multiply.

If the soil is not loose and able to breathe, then the anaerobic microbes (microbes which do not need air to grow) present in the atmosphere will thrive. If this happens, the anaerobic microbes will break down the ingredients of your soil and produce toxic conditions, and your plants will not grow as well as they should, if at all.

You can understand then why we use this particular combination of ingredients for our standard soil mixture. The ability to drain water is of primary concern as is the ability to hold and properly release the nutrients. You will also find that this soil mixture will not harden or crust.

You should test the pH of your soil once every three weeks or so. When you do this, first be sure to test the pH of the water you are watering the soil with.

Other Mediums

I often use "root cubes" (i.e. Jiffy 7 Pellets, Oasis cubes), available at most nurseries or garden stores. We not only use them for rooting, we also use them to start our seeds. The root cubes we will be using are sold in a variety of forms and sizes. Some are plain with a neutral pH. Other root cubes may contain nutrients for seedlings already inside. Others have the proper nutrient formulation specifically for rooting. These also have a neutral pH.

Whether you are planning to use a soil mixture or non-soil medium, be sure to check the pH. This is especially true if you are using Rockwool.

I have found that 2/3 vermiculite and 1/3 standard soil mixture works well for the clones. (I have even had success with 100% vermiculite). It seems to work better than the standard soil mixture (which I still recommend for all stages of growth). The vermiculite seems to allow the clones to "breathe" more efficiently.

This does not mean that there are not many other mediums or soil mixtures that will work just as well. We have tried to develop a happy medium between what is best and suitable, with what is standard and available. It is beyond the scope of this book to describe the Sea of Green as applied to a hydroponic garden (which produces a harsh smoke, in my opinion). Anyone interested in growing in a water-based system should purchase a book dedicated to hydroponics and apply those techniques to the Sea of Green method.

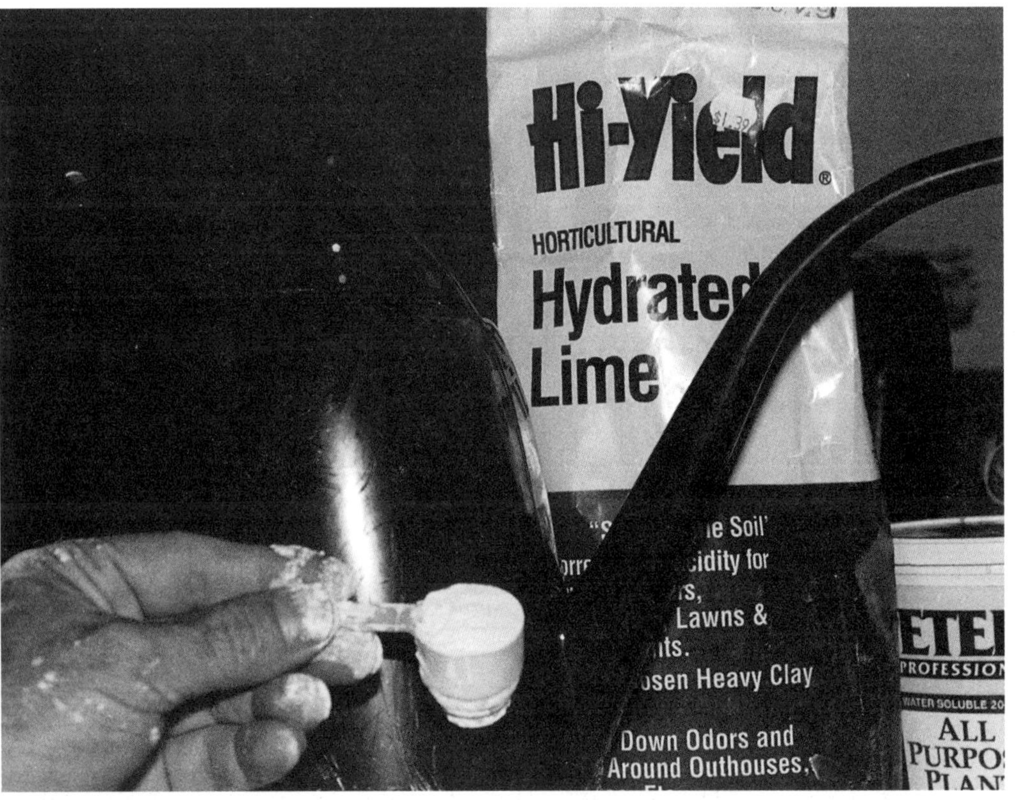

ADDING HYDRATED LIME TO THE WATER BEFORE GIVING IT TO THE PLANTS WILL HELP BALANCE THE PH. IT'S ALSO ADVISABLE TO TEST THE PH OF THE WATER. DO NOT USE MORE THAN ONE CUP OF HYDRATED LIME PER CUBIC FOOT OF SOIL.

pH

The pH factor is simply the balance between the acidity and the alkalinity of the soil. It may also be referred to as the chemical balance or charge of the soil.

The pH scale is measured from 1 to 14. The reading of 1 is the most acidic. As the number increases, it indicates that the soil is less acidic until you reach 7, which is neutral. The number 8 is the least alkaline measurement for soil, and number 14 is the most alkaline.

There are a few ways to measure the pH. Litmus paper is the most common, simple and inexpensive method. To take a pH reading using litmus paper, place a sample of the soil to be tested into a container, then saturate the soil with distilled water (measure the water beforehand to make sure it has a neutral pH). Place two pieces of litmus paper into the wet soil. After 10 seconds remove one of the litmus pieces and check it against the color chart which comes with the litmus paper. Then wait 10 more seconds and remove the other piece, and check it against the color chart.

I suggest using a pH meter (**see photo**). It's inexpensive, gives an immediate response, is easy to read, and its long probe allows you to easily check the pH of the bottom as well as the top of your containers. This is very handy when you want to check the bottom of the 5-gallon container which houses your "mammas."

Marijuana thrives best in a pH ranging from 6.0 to 8.0. Of course this means the pH you will seek to maintain at all times is 7.0. As long as all of the other major environmental conditions are met you can have a slight variance of pH either way and still have a successful crop. Do, however, attempt to maintain as near to 7.0 as you possibly can. This is a consistent pH for all stages of growth for your water and soil. This means that seedlings, clones, mammas and flowering plants should all be kept at this level.

Use horticultural hydrated lime to change the pH of your soil or water. If you add about three cups of hydrated lime to each cubic foot of soil you will raise the pH approximately 1 point. If you want to change the pH of your soil by watering, place about 1 cup of hydrated lime into a gallon of water and give your plant a standard watering. Lime stabilizes the soil because it has a neutral pH of 7.

If the pH is too high or too low, adjust it once, wait for 10 days and test it again. If you are close to a 7.0 pH, you won't need to adjust any more. You should not have to adjust the pH of your soil more than twice. However, if you're experiencing problems, remember that you must keep the pH of the soil near the neutral 7.0, even if this means having to check it once every two weeks.

A PH METER, AS PICTURED BELOW, WILL SHOW THE PH FOR ALL STAGES OF A PLANT'S GROWTH. THE PH FACTOR IS THE MEASURE OF THE SOIL'S ACID OR ALKALINE CONTENT. A PH FACTOR OF 6.5 TO 7 IS BEST.

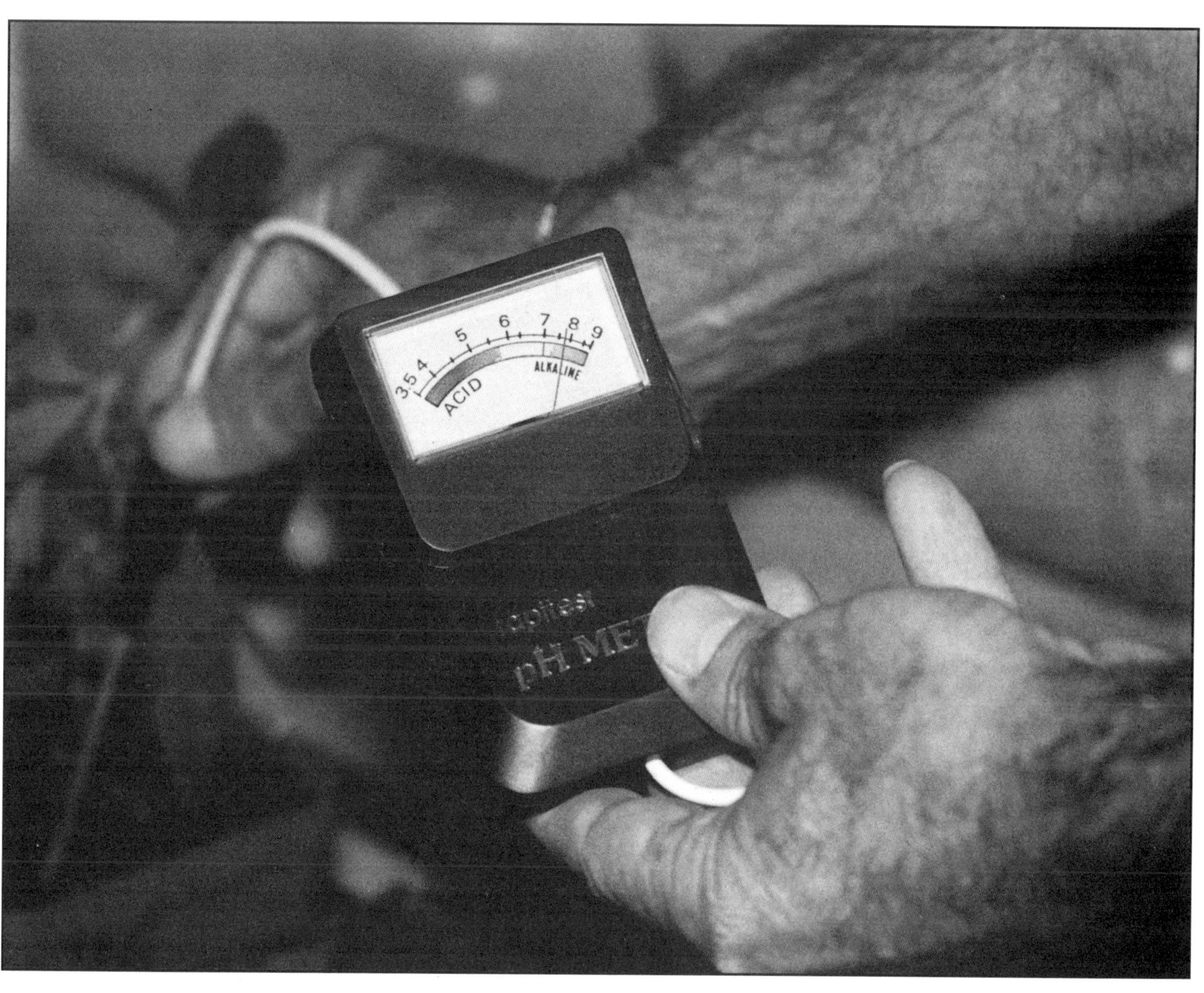

WATER

Water enters the plant via the root system along with nutrients and oxygen. It travels up the stalk, through the limbs and finally to the leaves. This flow is called the transpiration stream. The water is utilized by the plant before carrying unwanted waste out in a process called transpiration. It holds the plant upright and rigid and assists in photosynthesis. Without this precious fluid there would be no pot.

If you are concerned that your water may contain too much chlorine, place it in an open container for a few days and let the chlorine evaporate. If you find the pH of your water is not correct, you may correct it with the addition of horticultural hydrated lime. Simply add a tablespoon of lime to each gallon of water, stir vigorously and test. Add more or less lime until the desired pH is obtained. Then water.

Watering Tips

Well water is usually the best for watering. I have also seen marijuana exhibit growth spurts when watered with collected rainwater.

You should refrain from using water that has been pumped through a water softener. This will add salts to your water that are harmful to your plants. If your water goes through one of these softeners, intercept it before entering and obtain it there.

I have found that it is best to water your plants early in their day (when their light cycle begins). This way, the water has a chance to interact with the plant during the normal course of the plant's day. It also helps for the water to evaporate by the day's end, which means the plants will be drier during the night when they are more likely to mold or develop fungus. Any regular misting should be done in the morning hours for this reason. You should not mist your plants late in the evening or right before their lights go off.

If you have the extra bucks you may want to consider a moisture meter. They may be found for about $30 or $40. A good investment, they will tell you what you can't see under the soil.

Your watering requirements will differ according to the stage of growth. When you are starting your seedlings you will want to keep the growing medium (soil, root cubes, etc.) saturated until the seeds actually germinate. Once the seeds sprout and the roots begin to form, the seeds' growing medium must be kept moist at all times, but conversely you must allow the soil to dry out a little bit at times. The same is true for the other stages of plant growth. After the clones are placed in soil, they need this same drying-out period, then a watering, then drying, etc. The plants in the blooming room and the mammas will need to breathe the same way with this cycle of watering and drying.

When your clones are in their medium and waiting to grow roots remember to have at least 1" of standing water in the trays at all times for at least the first 6 to 8 days after the initial cloning. Be sure that the water in the trays is changed once every 48 hours during those 6 to 8 days.

When you are watering, try and water around the rim of your containers and not on the stem of the plant. Since the roots form towards the rim of the soil containers, this will deliver more water to the plant.

Overwatering

Overwatering is a common problem. If you are not sure that a plant needs water, don't water. You can find out how long a plant can go without watering by simply not watering your plants, and then measuring exactly how long it takes before they start to wilt. You should not let all of your plants wilt each time before you water but doing this once or twice will give you an insight into the requirements of whatever breed of plant you are growing. You will be able to look at certain plants, remember when you last watered them and know when they will need water again. After a while you will be able to lift a certain container and determine by the weight of the container how much moisture is present. These insights will come with practice.

If you slant your tables or racks in the blooming area one inch toward the edge you tend them on, any excess water will flow to the lower end where it may be readily spotted and removed with a large turkey baster.

The larger your room and the more plants you have, the more water you will have to deliver. For a small closet setup, a watering can will do. For larger setups (several hundred plants), a rubber hose will save a lot of time. For one large room I purchased a six-foot long PVC pipe with a foot-long perpendicular attachment that was very helpful in reaching the plants and pouring water into the tops of the containers.

Sometimes, a grow room will not have access to nearby water, and you will have to carry it in. This should be avoided, but for security reasons it's sometimes necessary. I have, at times, carried 5-gallon containers under cover of darkness to certain locations. The water was then placed in a large, clean, sturdy, plastic garbage can, and a properly-sized fish aquarium water heater was used to keep the water the right temperature until it was needed. (I once used this method successfully for a grow room that lost its water supply due to a winter freeze.)

DIFFERENT STAGES OF GROWTH WILL HAVE DIFFERENT WATERING REQUIREMENTS. SEEDS NEED TO BE KEPT ALMOST TOTALLY SATURATED UNTIL THEY SPROUT. CLONES WILL REQUIRE A LOT OF STANDING WATER. BUT AS THEY MATURE, THEIR NEEDS FOR WATER WILL LESSEN.

Ten Watering Tips

1. City and well water often contains contaminants that affect plant growth. Allowing water to sit will remove chlorine. To remove other impurities (organics, chloramines, phosphate complexes and undissolved solids), a water filtration system should be used. Running water through an ion-exchange absorber, then a water filter, will purify water.

2. Don't forget to test the pH of the water before using it on the plants. It should be in the 6.5 to 7 range.

3. A reservoir system, made of dark plastic to discourage algae growth, is recommended by many growers. A cheap reservoir system can be made from a large garbage can. This gives more control over the quality of the water you're giving the plants.

4. A marijuana plant will probably survive underwatering but can die from overwatering. The roots need to breathe and too much water will choke them.

5. When watering the plants, make sure the water is seeping down into the soil. Too often, the water will run over the surface of the container without reaching the roots.

6. A pump system may be necessary in some areas to get water to the plants. A hand pump can be enough for a small garden. A solar battery or even a wind-powered system can also be hooked up to a water pump.

7. Never use water that has been processed by a water softener. It contains salt, which is deadly to plants.

8. If you want to be absolutely sure that the plants are receiving enough water, a moisture meter ($10-30) will indicate exactly how much moisture soil contains at any point. Using a moisture meter will not disturb the plant's root system the way a finger will.

9. Running a hose into a garden can save a lot of time. If the hose is attached to a faucet that can control water temperature, it will be easier to give your plants tepid water. Be sure the hose has an on/off control, but try to turn it off at the source to avoid leaks.

10. A common cause of overwatering is poor ventilation. Unless the plants can breathe properly, they won't be able to process water.

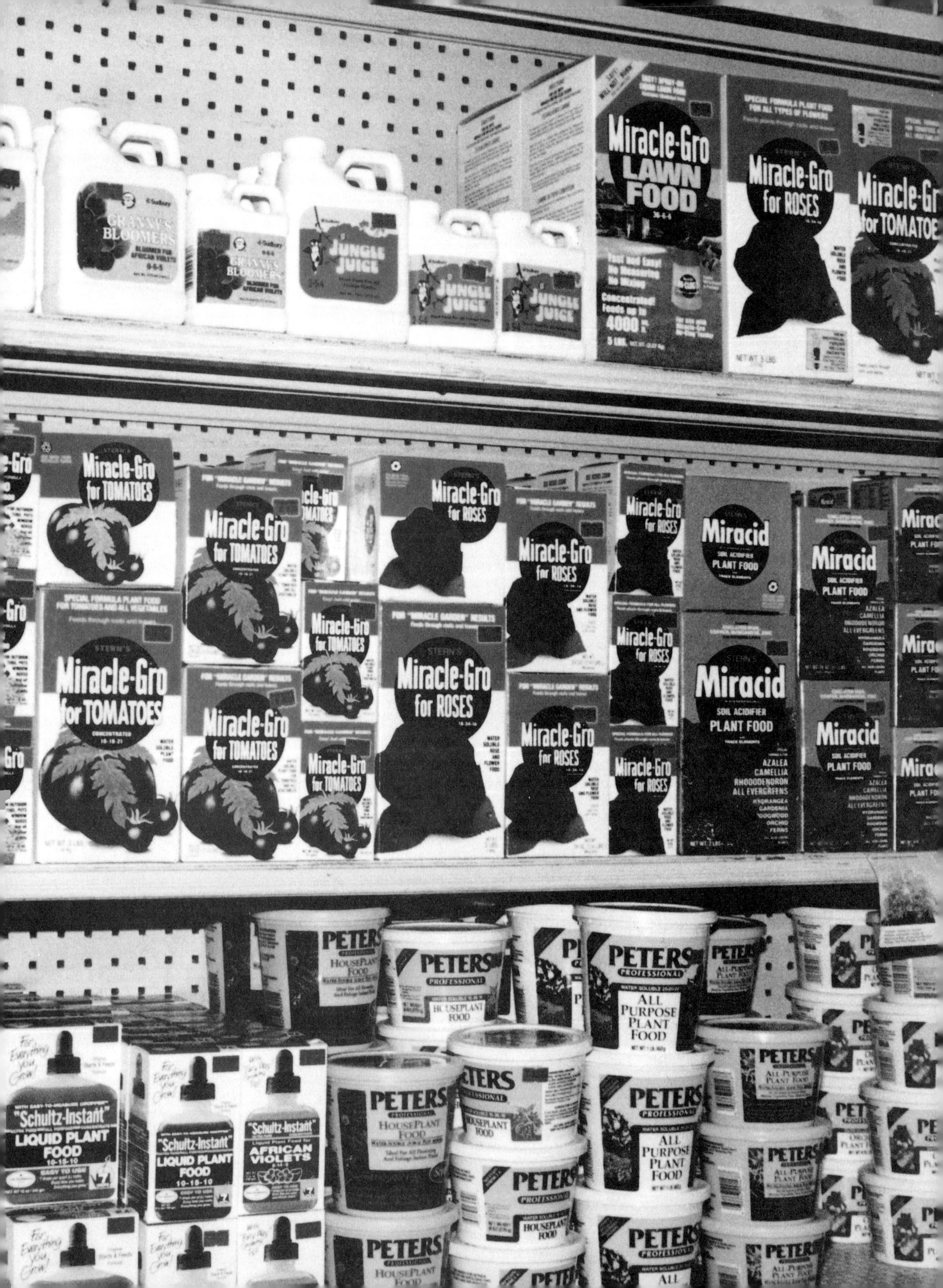

GRANNY'S BLOOMERS
JUNGLE JUICE
Miracle-Gro LAWN FOOD
Miracle-Gro for ROSES
Miracle-Gro for TOMATOES
Miracid SOIL ACIDIFIER PLANT FOOD
AZALEA CAMELLIA RHODODENDRON ALL EVERGREENS
PETERS PROFESSIONAL
HOUSEPLANT FOOD
ALL PURPOSE PLANT FOOD
For Everything you Grow!
"Schultz-Instant" LIQUID PLANT FOOD 10-15-10
"Schultz-Instant" AFRICAN VIOLETS

FERTILIZATION

Organic fertilizers are suitable for growing marijuana: worm castings, cow manure, horse manure, bat guano, chicken manure, fish emulsion, bone meal etc. One of the advantages of using organic fertilizers is that they are less likely to "burn" your plants because they are, for the most part, less concentrated than chemical fertilizers, so they release their energy at a slower rate. Some release energy faster than others. For example, corn stalks break down slowly whereas chicken manure breaks down very rapidly. Wood ash and bone meal are faster-acting than blood meal and cottonseed meal.

Organic fertilizers help to condition your soil medium because their mass helps to hold water. I suggest using limited amounts of worm castings and pasteurized cow manure. We do not suggest that you use large amounts of organic fertilizers, especially if you are not an experienced grower. If you do not mix your soil properly you may not achieve the proper water drainage. Stick to the standard soil mixture I outlined in the chapter on "Soil." Once you become more familiar with the growing process you should experiment with different fertilizers.

Organic Fertilizers

The first alternate fertilizer I would recommend is fish emulsion. It is water-soluble, and if you follow the dosage instructions on the package, quite simple to use. It comes in a variety of concentrations of different nutrients.

If you are going to use organic fertilizers be sure they are clean and free of bugs.

I suggest the use of high nitrogen fish emulsion for the mother plants.

Be careful using something as hot as chicken manure. Start with about 5% and work your way up to a bigger percentage once you have had time to measure the results from a small amount.

Bat guano is often mentioned by other growers, but I don't like it. I don't like the fact that it carries an unreasonable amount of bacteria, and possibly viruses. My suggestions for the best organic fertilizers for indoor marijuana cultivation are cow manure and worm castings.

You can make a "tea" of organic items such as chicken manure, horse manure, etc. Simply place a measured amount of substance in a container, add ample water and let the mixture sit, or "brew," overnight. Drain the mixture through a fine mesh the next day and water moderately. Check the results. If you used 2 gallons of water and 2 gallons of organic material on 10 plants and the mixture did not burn them, try using the same amount on 8 plants.

The leftover organic material should be discarded, although it can be added to the soil for any outdoor plants, as it will slowly release any remaining nutrients into the soil. Although fertilizer "tea" is best suited for outdoor growing, it can come in handy for indoor use. However, buying organic fertilizers from a commercial outlet can become expensive.

If you live in a rural area, it can be easy to obtain chicken or horse manure. If you live near a horse stable, it can be hauled away for free, or for a nominal fee (like $5 a truckload).

Chemical Fertilizers

Chemical fertilizers are usually faster-acting than organics due to the fact that all their ingredients are in a water soluble form. For this reason you must be careful not to overfertilize when using them. There are a variety of chemical fertilizers that you may use; some are in liquid form, some are granular, and some are in powder form. Some are acid and some are alkaline. We will again try and find the happy balance between requirements and availability.

Marijuana plants require a full-spectrum fertilizer that contains all the primary nutrients (nitrogen, phosphorous and potassium) as well as secondary nutrients (calcium, sulfur and magnesium) and trace elements (boron, copper, iron, manganese, zinc, and molybdenum). Using these will give your plants the "full spectrum" of necessary nutrients for proper growth. There are many commercial companies which produce these. I suggest purchasing old standbys such as Miracle-Gro, Ra-Pid-Gro or Hydro-Gro. These are all easy-to-find, commercial products, available at most garden stores.

If you can't find a full-spectrum fertilizer at your local garden or hardware store, you may supplement your regular fertilizer with special trace element fertilizers. These are solutions that are primarily composed of secondary and trace elements. I use F.T.E., manufactured by the same company I buy the potting soil from (Peters), and recommended it for use with standard Peter's formulas. The company also makes S.T.E.M. and Compound III, but I have found that the F.T.E. is slow-releasing. A quick-releasing fertilizer like Peters' S.T.E.M. is easily overused. Ask your local nursery staff for help in locating these or any other fertilizers in your area if they do not keep them in stock.

There is organic fertilizer in my suggested standard soil mixture, but only a small amount, as well as Super Thrive (a vitamin and hormone supplement manufactured by Vitamin Institute) and B1 (a vitamin that helps spur root growth, available from Ortho, Safers, Shultz and other companies). From my experience, organic fertilizers alone do not have all the secondary and trace elements necessary to produce truly healthy marijuana plants and the biggest, most potent marijuana flowers, unless you use a mixture of the right organics. This is not for the novice. If you want to go completely organic, I suggest you get some experience first.

The reason we want a full-spectrum fertilizer is because the soil medium we will be using is not your standard dirt taken from the ground. It is a manmade soil made up of potting soil, perlite and some worm castings. But we need to replenish the soil with fertilizer for many reasons. High-grade marijuana needs a lot of fertilizer—it uses a lot of energy. The constant watering will also leach some of the nutrients out of the soil. The small containers we will be using rapidly fill up with the growing root systems, which will utilize the soil nutrients quickly. For these reasons we will periodically need to replenish the growing medium with a full spectrum of nutrients.

The mammas will be growing in your room longer than any of the other plants so they will need a constant supply of all necessary nutrients. I like to give them a full-spectrum fertilizing about once every 5 or 6 weeks. For regular fertilizing of the mammas I like to use a standard application of a high-nitrogen fish-base emulsion.

Fertilizers are described by the use of three main indicators, designating the amount of each ingredient present.

Primary Nutrients

The three primary ingredients (a.k.a. major nutrients) of chemical fertilizers are listed as N-P-K. These initials stand for:

N: Nitrogen
P: Phosphorus
K: Potassium

These elements might be listed in a weak concentration such as N-2, P-1, K-1, or a stronger concentration such as N-20, P-15, K-15. The numbers designate the percentage of "primary nutrients" in the fertilizer.

NITROGEN (N) is the most important nutrient. Marijuana uses large amounts of nitrogen, so you will want to use a fertilizer with a high nitrogen content such as 20-15-15 or 20-15-10. Nitrogen is important in the makeup of amino acids and chlorophyll as well as assisting in leaf and stem growth and the overall well-being of a plant. Nitrogen is required most when the plant is in the vegetative state.

PHOSPHORUS (P) is also used in large quantities by marijuana. Phosphorus is essential for photosynthesis, respiration and the transfer of genes. Marijuana uses phosphorus mostly during the production of seeds when it is flowering. It also uses a lot for germination, seed development, resin production and cloning.

POTASSIUM or POTASH (K) is used to make a plant disease-resistant. It is also necessary for the making of sugars and starches, helps in photosynthesis and respiration, and is necessary for strong root growth.

YOU WILL NEED A BLOOMING FERTILIZER AND A VEGETATIVE FERTILIZER. PLANTS HAVE DIFFERENT NUTRITIONAL NEEDS AT DIFFERENT STAGES OF THEIR GROWTH. THIS ORCHID BLOOMING FORMULA WILL HELP CANNABIS FLOWERS AS WELL.

Secondary Nutrients

These are the secondary nutrients (a.k.a. macronutrients) found in commercial fertilizers:

CALCIUM (Ca) is used in mitosis and a small amount must be present at the growing tip of each root.

MAGNESIUM (Mg) is necessary for light absorption and is the central atom in chlorophyll.

Trace Elements

Trace elements (a.k.a. micronutrients) are used as catalysts. They assist with the translocation of energy, molecular processes and many of the other processes involved with the plant's life.

The trace elements are:

Copper (Cu)
Iron (Fe)
Boron (B)
Molybdenum (Mo)
Zinc (Zn)
Sulfur (S)

When following the standard Sea of Green procedure, you should not have any problems with deficiencies of the trace elements.

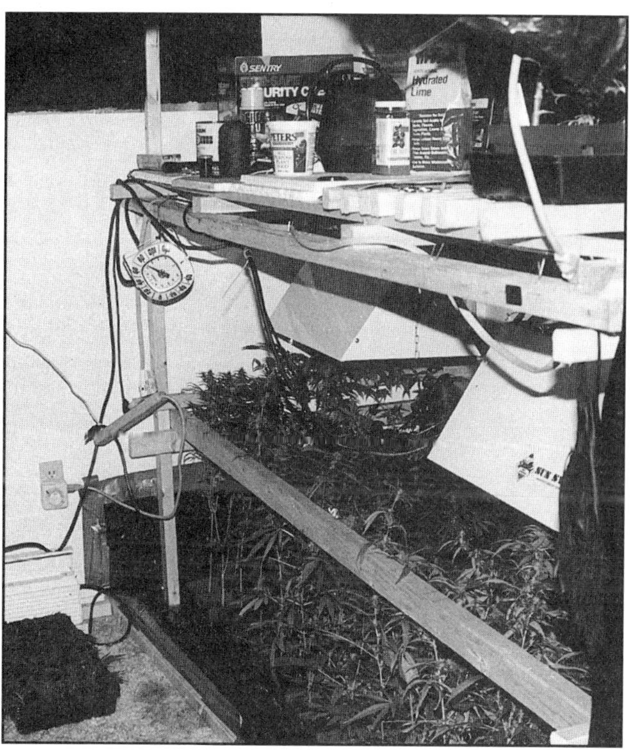

BUILDING A TABLE IN THE GROW ROOM IMPROVES LIGHTING EFFICIENCY AND CREATES MORE WORKING SPACE. IT CAN EVEN BE USED FOR STORAGE OF FERTLIZER AND NUTRIENT CONTAINERS.

When to Fertilize

One of the easiest things to do is overfertilize, especially when using chemical fertilizers. It can happen because you can't see whether the fertilizer is working or not and once you put a certain amount of fertilizer in the soil it is hard to tell whether it was too much or too little.

To avoid this, set up and maintain a standard fertilizing schedule—as recommended by the directions on the fertilizer package. Usually they will recommend that fertilization is required once every two weeks, but you may find that your plants will need fertilizing every three weeks, or half a fertilizing every two weeks. This is something that you will learn after you have worked with your crop over a period of time. If you follow the standard instructions in the second part of the book, you should be close to a normal and accurate fertilizing schedule.

My rule of thumb is: Fertilize less, more often. One way to avoid overdoing it is to cut the amount of recommended fertilization in half, but to apply it more often. For instance, if a container says to add 2 tablespoons to one gallon of water and fertilize once every two weeks, break that down and add one tablespoon (or even a half-tablespoon) to a gallon of water and add it once a week. Remember that this water will be for more than one plant. A plant in a 5 1/4" square will only get about a cup from the mixed gallon. On the other hand, a 5-gallon mamma container will get a quart of the same mixture.

If you aren't sure whether your plants need fertilizing or not, they probably don't. You should wait until you start to see the signs of underfertilization: yellowing of leaves or a pale green color. After a while you will learn to watch for the signs that indicate your fertilizer is working—leaves turning a darker, healthy green and an increase in growth rate. After a while you will be able to determine the amount of fertilizer you should use at any given time just by following these indicators.

The telltale signs that a plant is receiving too much nitrogen are that a plant will show a spurt of growth, turn a deep green color, then the tips of the leaves will curl under and turn yellow. In general, severely curly leaves or bending indicates severe overfeeding.

I prefer to use the type of fertilizer that is mixed with water rather than pellets or granules that are mixed in the soil, or broadcast on top of the soil. A fertilizer mixed in water will immediately be available to the plant, as it saturates the soil quickly and thoroughly. The results of the fertilization are therefore more apparent earlier, and there is less danger of overfeeding the plants. Most chemical fertilizers are mixed with water, while organics are usually mixed with the soil, unless an extraction (or "tea") is made with them.

You should never fertilize your plants if the soil is too dry. If it is, then figure out how much water your plants need and water them with half of it. Then fertilize the plants with the soluble fertilizer mixed with the other half for a regular watering.

Deficiencies

Sometimes the soil becomes deficient in some nutrient(s), usually one of the primary ones. This can be corrected with a standard fertilization.

The second most common nutrient deficiency is magnesium, which is why hydrated lime was added to the standard soil mixture. To overcome this deficiency, two heaping tablespoons of fine dolomite lime can be added to the standard soil mixture. The slow-releasing dolomite lime is a combination of magnesium (Mg) and calcium (Ca), and is a fine complement to the faster-releasing hydrated lime.

One of the main concerns regarding plants and nutrients is the pH. If the pH is not properly balanced, nutrients will not be available to the plants. You will add more nutrients, but your plant will become overfertilized.

A good way to add balance to the process is to develop a fertilizing standard. Use the standard, well-rounded fertilizer such as 10-5-5 (for vegetative growth), or 20-20-20. This way you will be assured of getting all adequate nutrients besides nitrogen (which is all there would be in a 10-0-0).

The same is true with the blooming fertilizer. Don't use a 0-0-5 if you want a well-rounded concentration of nutrients and are worried about having too much of one nutrient.

You can use almost any brand-name fertilizer or plant food for your plants.

A good method for nutrient observation is to have one or two test plants. Give one plant one-quarter to one-half <u>more</u> fertilizer than normal, then give another plant one-quarter to one-half <u>less</u> than a standard application (the directions on the label). Watch what happens to both plants and meter your next fertilizations based on your observation of those results to determine if the standard application is too much or too little. (We suggest that you calculate the recommended dosage of fertilizer and give half doses in two-week intervals and adjust from there.)

THESE PRE-FLOWERS ARE A HEALTHY, DARK GREEN COLOR, AND THE LEAVES ARE SMOOTH AND STURDY. THIS IS INDICATIVE OF PROPER FERTILIZATION. ON THE OTHER HAND, IF THE PLANTS HAD DARK GREEN VEINS AND LIGHT GREEN TISSUE IT WOULD INDICATE A PHOSPHOROUS DEFICIENCY. CURLING LEAVES SOMETIMES INDICATE A LACK OF OXYGEN AT THE ROOT LEVEL.

GERMINATING THE SEEDS

TOP: Once you have secured seed stock, purchased the necessary equipment, and set up the grow room areas you will be ready to begin. TOP: Examine your seeds very closely and choose the best-looking ones to begin your project. LOWER LEFT AND RIGHT: To germinate the seeds, plant them in small 2 1/4"peat moss containers. Use chopstick or other pointed object to make a hole to drop the seed in. Don't put the seed at the bottom of the container—leave about a quarter-inch of space for the roots and water the soil until it's saturated. Continue to water every day.

TRANSPLANTATION

TOP LEFT: Once the seeds have sprouted, it's time to transplant them into larger 5 1/4" containers.
TOP RIGHT, CENTER AND BOTTOM: Scoop up the seedling and the surrounding dirt with a spoon and gently place into the larger container.
BOTTOM LEFT: Pat the soil down, and water.
LEFT CENTER: If the seed is germinated in a small peat moss cup, the entire cup can be placed in the larger container.

THE CLONING PROCEDURE

AT RIGHT: Using a knife or sharp scissors, cut the top three or four inches off the plant—just above the node. **ABOVE RIGHT:** Immediately dip the plant into rooting solution, and replant the cutting into a soil container. **ABOVE CENTER:** Place the freshly-cut clone into a 5 1/4" soil-filled container. **ABOVE BOTTOM:** Pat down the dirt surrounding the clone. After this point, place the clones under fluorescent light for 18 hours a day. After two weeks they will develop roots of their own.

PREFLOWERING

TOP RIGHT AND CENTER: The purpose of the preflowering area is to grow the clones a large as possible (usually 12 to 18 inches). Some growers give preflowers 24 hours c light, but 18 hours per day is usually sufficient. **RIGHT CENTER:** Check your preflower every day to see if they need watering. When clones are first transplanted, they wi need a lot of watering to encourage development of roots, but once they are moved int the preflowering area their water needs will not be as great. The best time to water i early in their day, when they first receive light. **AT LEFT AND CENTER RIGHT:** In sma closet systems, preflowers and mother plants can be kept in the same area of the grov room. Because the mother plant will always be in the vegetative stage of growth, bot mammas and preflowers will thrive under 18 hours of MH light.

ORTHO
UP-START

THE BLOOMING AREA

ALL PHOTOS THIS PAGE: Once clones are placed in the blooming area, where they receive only 12 hours a day from a metal halide or high-pressure sodium light, they will begin to form buds. It takes anywhere from 8-12 weeks for most varieties of cannabis to complete the flowering cycle. By rotating clones in various stages of growth, the Sea of Green "perpetual harvest" assures that buds can be harvested every two to three weeks.

Sea Of Green

Tips For Fertilization

1. Most plants will not suffer from nutrient deficiencies if they are planted in fresh potting soil that is fortified with the right fertilizer.

2. If a plant does not have enough nutrients, the plant's leaves will be a lime green color. An application of a general-purpose fertilizer will usually solve the problem.

3. If a plant has received too many nutrients (i.e. too much fertilizer), the plant's leaves (often the lower leaves) will be a dark green color. Leaching the soil (cleaning it by watering thoroughly), or transplanting plants into fresh soil containers, will solve the problem.

4. Often, signs of nutrient deficiency are actually due to an improper soil pH. Always test the soil pH before adding fertilizer.

5. If the soil's pH is over 8 or under 6, it's sometimes easier to change the soil than to try to adjust the pH.

6. Here are eight common signs of problems:

    1. Wilting: too hot, too dry, too much water.
    2. Plant growing slowly: too much water, too cold, not enough fertilizer.
    3. Brown leaf margins: air too hot and dry, too much water/fertilizer.
    4. Spots on leaves: spider mites or other pests, too much fertilizer.
    5. Yellow leaves that fall: not enough humidity, too much water, air too cold, not enough fertilizer.
    6. Yellow leaves that stay on: pH problem, water too hard (well water).
    7. Rotting plants: mold or fungus, too much water, too much humidity.
    8. Sudden dropping of leaves or buds: too much water, air too dry, air too cold, transplant shock.

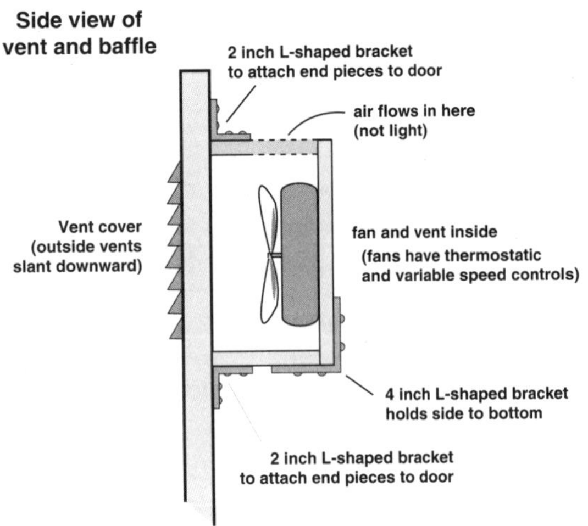

CLOSET VENTILATION SYSTEM

ENVIRONMENT

"At least the air is free." So it is said. Air also plays a very important part in the life of marijuana.

Marijuana plants derive air from their lowest level—the roots, where it is removed from the water. If no oxygen is present in the roots they cannot function. One of the functions of the root system is to help transport oxygen to the rest of the plant.

The plant also breathes through tiny openings in the outer layer of the leaf surface. These small pores (stomata) bring in oxygen (O_2) and carbon dioxide (CO_2) to the plant for a myriad of uses. These stomata must be clean at all times—dust, dirt and other foreign matter can clog them. When growing outdoors the wind and the rain clean the plant's leaves, but you will have to simulate these natural conditions in your growing area.

Whenever a pesticide is sprayed on the plants (my recommendations for their use are discussed in the next chapter), it should be sprayed off 24-48 hours after it has been applied to keep the stomata clean. Spraying the plants with a fine mist of water and thoroughly washing the plants will remove the bug pesticides. This will help the stomata to breathe. It does not hurt to give both sides of your leaves a fine-mist spraying each morning to remove dust and dirt.

Air Circulation

In whatever room or location you use, there must be air circulation. If the air is not circulating and air from outside is not getting in, the plants will not be getting the full benefit of fresh carbon dioxide and oxygen, both of which are necessary for any plant or animal. If the air doesn't move, an area of "dead" air forms around the leaf surface and the plant won't breathe properly—the stomata will be unable to take in fresh CO_2 and O_2. If this happens, a plant cannot properly utilize its food nor can it involve itself in the process of photosynthesis. Just as a human would get sick if he or she could not breathe properly, the plant's growth will become stunted or the plant will become "sick." Additionally, bugs, mold, temperature and humidity will be harder to control when air doesn't circulate. To grow healthy plants, fresh air must be present in an ever-replenished supply. The entire metabolism of the plant is dependent upon the movement of the air around it.

Another good reason for maximizing air circulation in the grow room is that hot air rises, while cold air settles to the floor. Installation of an oscillating fan in each separate area of your room will help your plants to breathe and give you a more even distribution of the temperature. Circulating air will also be less humid, which is important in helping to keep fungus and mold growth down. Still another reason is that CO_2, which is very important to plant growth, is heavier than air and will settle to the floor without circulation.

Fresh Air

You need to have an exhaust system in your growing area—whether it is something as simple as two open windows in a room for a closet system (with the door open), or a sophisticated central heating and/or cooling system that continually replenishes the room with fresh air adjusted to the perfect temperature, or even a CO_2 and O_2 system from an internal supply.

For large setups, I like to heat or cool the air in the cloning area of the room, then duct that air into the blooming area and then outside the grow rooms. I also screen all vents to keep bugs out. Air that is moving through a given area will not have as much O_2 or CO_2 on a day with no wind compared to a day with wind. Wind replenishes the ingredients available to the surface of a plant. Therefore, if you are bringing air into one end of your system at a slow rate, and exiting an equal amount of air from the other side of the area, then you will make enough usable components of the air available to the leaf surface.

Setting Up the Vent/Exhaust Fan

Fans come in many sizes and they are rated by their cfm: how many cubic feet per minute of air a fan is able to move through its blades. Any fan you purchase will have its cfm rating listed: buy one that is rated at least 1/5 the volume of the grow room, or as high as 1/2. A 12' long by 10' wide by

7' tall room is 840 cubic feet: the rating I would recommend for the room's fan would be 175 cfm minimum, 420 maximum. I like to have a fan which is two or three times the minimal requirement so if I want to evacuate the room's air as quickly as possible, I simply turn the fan's setting to the max. For instance, after using a pesticide you will want to clean the air very quickly. Sometimes I want to cool off or heat up the room temperature quickly, or dry it out.

You should place your fans at the top of any area you use. If you convey any air from one place to another, place the fan so that it is pulling the air out of an area rather than pushing it into an area. The reason is that it is easier on the fan because it is aerodynamically easier to pull air from an area rather than build up a lot of pressure to push air out of one area into another.

I like a fan that fits into the piping used on wood-burning stoves—they're cheap, versatile, and available in many sizes at most lumberyards. If an area calls for a 5" fan, this would always be my first choice. They will also fit into a flexible dryer hose—the pipe and the hose may be used as conduits for the tranfer of air from one place to another. The advantage of these two items is that they may be bent so that the light from one room does not leak into another—the conduit blocks the light but not the air flow. A flap on the exit end of the conduit will keep drafts and unwanted bugs from entering your project through the conduit.

"Squirrel cage" or "ram's horn" fans are also popular, but a little bit more expensive. These will also fit in a 4" diameter clothes-dryer exhaust-hose kit.

For large grow rooms, where a larger fan is needed (1280 cfm or more), check the Yellow Pages under "building supplies." For the greenhouse setup, I used an attic exhaust fan, which are popular in rural areas for cooling homes during summer months.

By using a variable-speed fan, I can turn a fan on or off when a suitable temperature is achieved and also exhaust the air at whatever rate I need. You can buy variable-speed, thermostat-controlled fans, but they are expensive. I prefer to take whatever fan I buy and add a "heavy duty" thermostat control as well as a "heavy duty" variable-speed control. (Make sure it says "heavy duty"—"standard" just isn't strong enough.) A thermostat control is a simple device that turns the fan on or off so you can, for instance, set the temperature to 80 degrees on and 74 degrees off. The variable speed control will simply set the fan on different speeds, but unlike the standard three-speed fan, there are no settings, just an adjustable speed dial. These devices are available at most stores that sell lamps, or any hardware store.

Of course, if there are neighbors around, the exhaust system will be pushing out skunky-smelling air. There are commercial products on the market that mask these smells. A negative air ionizer, available at hardware stores, has been very popular for years and will eliminate plant odors. An alternative available from a company called Ozone Environmental Technologies (1-800-765-2098) is a product called the Uvonair air deodorant and purification system, which is compact and energy-efficient. (As always, use discretion when calling—don't draw attention to why you need their product.)

INSTALLATION OF A SMALL EXHAUST FAN IS THE MOST IMPORTANT THING YOU CAN DO TO ENSURE GOOD VENTILATION. PLANTS NEED FRESH AIR TO THRIVE. A VARIABLE-SPEED FAN CAN HELP REGULATE ROOM TEMPERATURE. HOWEVER, BE SURE THAT THE FAN DOES NOT RELEASE THE AIR ANYWHERE THAT PEOPLE COULD DETECT THE PLANT ODOR.

Temperature

The room temperature is so important to the plants' growth and health that I keep my exhaust fan on a thermostat.

I try to keep the temperature at 75 to 80 degrees in the growing area. If the temperature is too low (i.e. 62 degrees), or too hot (i.e. 100 degrees), the plants won't grow as fast as they should. The perfect growth temperature is around 75 degrees, day or night.

In the wintertime you should not let the temperature of the grow area vary more than 15 degrees between lighting periods—this will stress your plant. Since it gets colder at night, in some grow setups (such as trailers or uninsulated sheds) it will be harder to maintain an even 76 degrees 24 hours a day. Regardless of the outside temperature, don't let the inside temperature drop more than 15 degrees.

This can become very difficult. When growing in a trailer setup, I once noticed that there was a difference of 8-10 degrees during the winter months between the temperature of the ceiling and that of the floor. This is an example of why I keep thermometers all over every room in different areas. Sometimes one specific part of the room will need to have the temperature adjusted. I also keep an indoor/outdoor thermometer in the grow area, which has a 6' wire with a temperature indicator at the end. I'll use one part of it to give me the temperature of the roof in a grow room and the 6' wire to tell me the temperature of the floor in the same room.

You must take into consideration the heat produced by your lights and ballasts. They can help heat the room during the winter months, but it will need to be cooled down in the summer. If you need more heat in your room at night you should consider setting up the plant-light cycle so that the lights are on during the coldest part of the night. (Warning: this can also make the room more easily detectable by law-enforcement infrared heat scanners.) Likewise, if you have too much heat from the lights during the summer months, you should set up the cycle so the lights are off during the hottest part of the day. Since this is a year-round system you should be prepared to both heat and cool your room.

EACH SEPARATE AREA OF THE GROW ROOM SHOULD HAVE A THERMOMETER. THAT WAY, YOU CAN LOCATE ANY HOT SPOTS, COLD DRAFTS, OR OTHER CONDITIONS THAT CAN INHIBIT GOOD PLANT GROWTH.

I like to cool with an air-conditioner and heat with either electricity or propane-gas. Propane has the added advantage of giving off CO_2 as a byproduct, which is very useful for increasing plant growth. You'll need to purchase a propane gas tank, a commercial heating unit, a few feet of hose and a regulator, which are usually available at your local hardware store, or even through a propane gas outlet (as in *King of The Hill*, the popular cartoon series). If you decide that a propane heater is right for your setup (usually best for a remote area, a trailer or an outdoor shed where central heating is not available), tanks of varying sizes may be obtained, and a salesperson will help you decide how large or small a heater you will need. (Of course, you will keep your activity confidential.)

Make sure you purchase a unit with a thermal coupling cutoff for the pilot light. This will automatically turn off the gas flow if the pilot light goes off. Do not hook up a gas tank to a heater without this safety device. To test the connection of your hose, regulator and heater, put a half-teaspoon of soap into a quart of water and place the mixture into a hand pump-sprayer set to "mist." Spray each gas connection. Any bubbles that form will indicate a gas leak. Most propane has a distinct odor, and will be easy to detect if you have a good sense of smell.

If you use electricity for heat, be sure not to overload the circuits, and don't use extension cords with electric heaters.

Humidity

As you know, marijuana is grown all over the world, from hot, arid desert regions such as the Middle East or Australia, to the steaming rainforests of Africa or Central America. Marijuana can grow in almost any climate on the planet. Although it can grow in many different levels of humidity, from deserts to jungles, we need to artificially create the ideal level.

Humidity is the amount of moisture in the atmosphere at a given temperature. The ability of the air to hold moisture approximately doubles for every increase of 20 degrees Fahrenheit.

Humidity affects the transpiration of the stoma. (Transpiration is the giving off of vapors which carry waste products out of the plant through its leaves.) Too high and it slows, too low and it slows. The relative humidity you will want to create is 50 to 70 percent. High humidity can also increase the likelihood of fungus and rot.

The best way to prevent high humidity is to use your exhaust fan properly. If you have a problem with too much humidity you may place a humidistat in line with your thermostat and whenever the humidity or temperature get too high, your vent fan is turned on until the proper conditions are obtained.

You may want to consider a dehumidifier, a commercial device available at your local hardware or department store. However, this will add to the electrical load, as they are costly.

On the other hand, if you live in an area where the air is very dry, you might consider the purchase of a humidifier, although the same results can be obtained by placing trays or buckets of water around the area and letting them evaporate.

The only times you will want the room humidity high is when you are germinating your seedlings and when your clones are rooting. You may want to mist rooting clones a few times a day if possible. Humidity of up to 75 percent is acceptable. A humidity dome of plastic can also be used.

If you are controlling the room temperature with a heater or air conditioner, remember that the air current from these devices is very dry, and this will affect your plants, especially if they are very young. Keep seedlings and clones away from the direct air flow.

Pruning

You will need to prune your plants during several different stages of the growing process.

1. Cut at the seedling stage

The first time you should prune your plants is right after you transplant your seedlings into the 5 1/4" squares. You should "pinch" the topmost growing tip—the very small 1/4" tip of the growing terminal—of each clone. Do this with scissors, a sharp razor blade or even a pair of garden shears.

Once the first terminal is removed, the plant will automatically reduce the amount of growth-inhibiting hormones present in the growing tips on the lower branches. This will increase growth of the entire plant, because the tips of the lower branches will begin to grow as if they were the topmost growing terminal. I prefer a clean, single-edge razor blade for this operation.

The reason you will do this with the seedlings is that once you determine their gender you will be using the best females for your stock of mother plants, and these will produce your supply of fresh clones, so you want as many healthy branches and tips as possible. If you start pinching the plants right away, they will evolve into the many-topped, squat bushes you want them to be. The reason for this is that after you pinch the first growing tip you will have at least two growing tips within 10 days. If you pinch both of these, within another 10 days you will have at least four growing tips. Keep this up and soon you will have a plant which will give you as many growing tips as you wish.

For best results, you need to remove only the top 1/4" or so of the tip of the growing terminal. This is why I use the word "pinch."

2. Trim the mother plant(s)

Once you have obtained the growth rate that you wish and are getting about 20 clones per plant every two weeks, keep only a few more branches than you need for clone production. By trimming the lower branches and leaves—any of the plant's weaker growth—the mother plant can devote its energies to the tips you want for clones. Remove branches in the middle of the plant that won't receive much light or point towards the main stem, since these won't be of much use to you and just use up the mamma's energy. If two branches are growing close to each other, cut off the smaller one. When you remove excess branches, you should trim the plant so that any remaining branches point away and are evenly spaced. If you want each plant to produce 10 clones every two weeks, prune the excess branches, and leave only the best 10. Remember to trim unnecessary tips of the mother plant whenever you do a cloning.

While you should always leave only as many terminals as you need on any given mother plant, I strongly advise that you clone all of them, and cut them almost all the way down to the "nubs." They will then grow back properly.

3. Careful pruning of clones

Once your plants have been placed in the blooming room you should do only a minimal amount of trimming. You especially do not want to remove any of the "fan" or "food" leaves of the clones. Some people trim these, thinking that the plant will get more light if they remove the leaves that are "in the way of the light." However, when you remove these leaves, you take away the part of the plant that uses light—these "food" leaves nourish the rest of the plant. You should remove any dying lower leaves or lower branches that look like they won't amount to anything.

There are some plant "bandages" that you might consider using when cutting off the larger branches, such as a drop of honey or a ball of warm beeswax, but usually the plant will take care of itself. Marijuana plants will secrete a translucent, yellow or red sap that acts as a natural protection. If a plant has more branches than you need, it shouldn't hurt the plant to cut them off, no matter what their size.

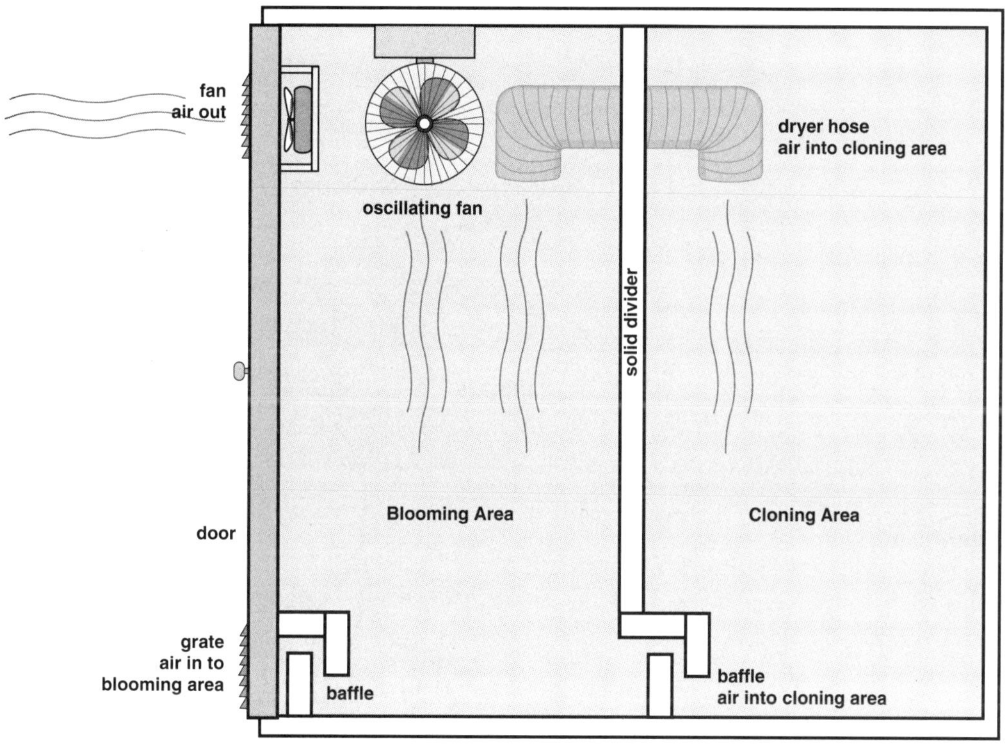

Inside View Closet
Side View

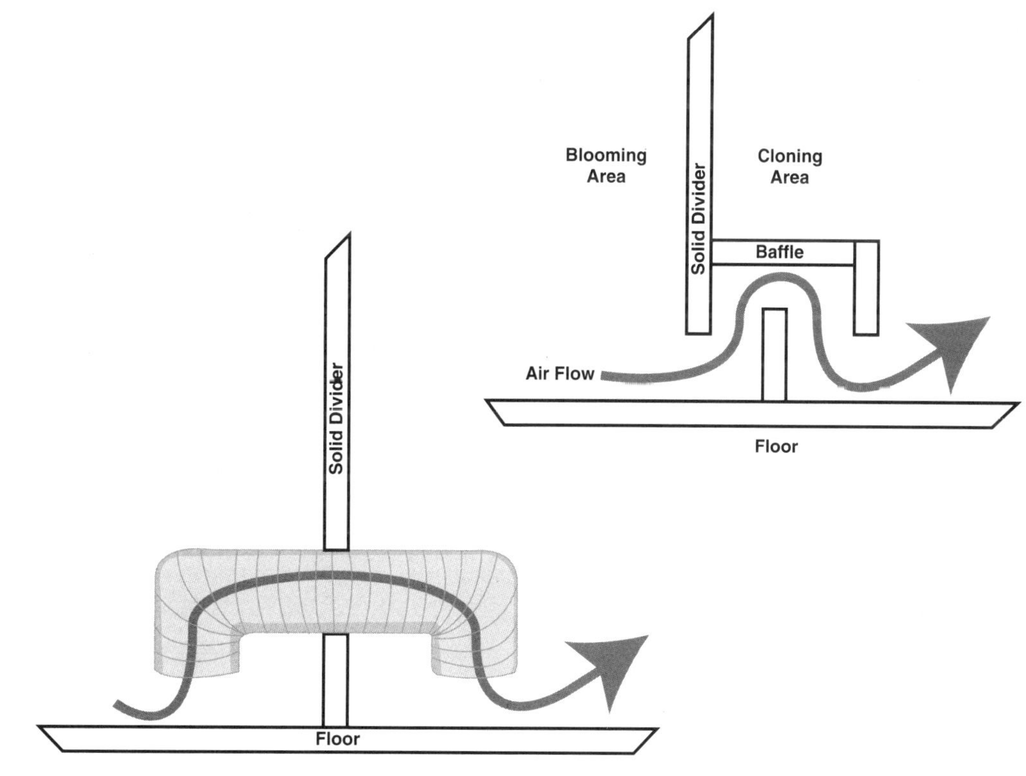

CLOSET VENTILATION SCHEME

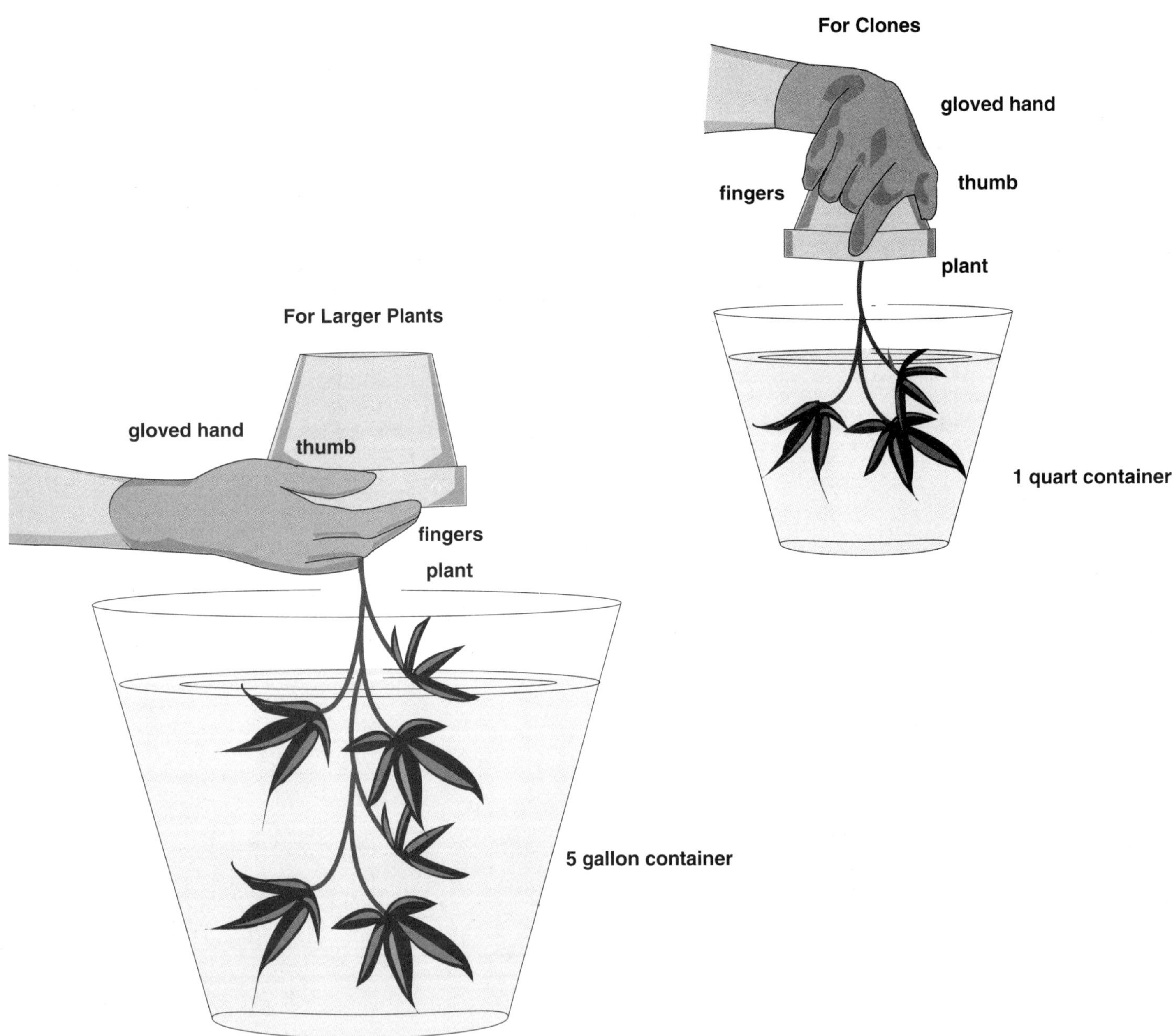

THE PLANT-DIP METHOD

PESTS

When growing in an enclosed, controlled environment you will usually have no problems with outside predators. But even with the best care and best intentions, sometimes you find them—bugs! Don't panic, don't trash your crop, don't worry. They can be controlled and eradicated.

Preventative Maintenance

Your best line of defense is preventative maintenance. This begins with you! When you visit your area, don't bring any bugs with you. Pests may be hidden in the clothes that you're wearing. They could sneak in on your muddy shoes. I visit my plants in the morning just after my morning shower, dressed in fresh, clean clothes. I do all standard maintenance right away.

When you first put your grow room together—and before anything organic goes into it—you should set off an insecticide aerosol. This will kill anything in the area and start you off fresh as far as bugs are concerned.

Any item that you bring into the area you are growing in should be cleaned. Wash your hands before entering the room. Any and all tools used for gardening should be washed and even sprayed with an insecticide before bringing them into the room. Once you bring them inside, don't take them out and in again; leave them in there. Items such as plastic trays or containers should be inspected before bringing them into the room.

The soil ingredients, such as potting soil and perlite, must be checked to make sure they're free of pests and fungus. If you are not sure about your soil medium, moisten it, then pour it into trays. Place the trays into a preheated oven at about 160-170 degrees and "cook" for 45 minutes to an hour. This will kill any pests that might be lurking in your soil.

You only really need to visit your plants a few times a day. The fewer visits, the less likely you are to carry any pests with you. This is, of course, up to each individual. There are some growers who automate their entire system so that they only need to visit once every two weeks to harvest (or even less often, if they aren't using the Sea of Green method). I prefer to visit twice a day—once in the morning, right before the lights go off, to attend to water, room temperature, nutrients, whatever. I think most grow rooms require two visits a day. If you can visit your crop more often, you should. If a serious problem should develop (for instance, the heating system breaks down in the wintertime or a bug infestation occurs), the sooner it is fixed, the better. You could lose the entire crop if the problem continues for a few days.

I keep a large, strong magnifying glass in the room. A daily inspection of your plants can be helpful in preventing a bug infestation. You should look on the undersides of the leaves and into the crevices formed at the nodes along the stems. A pair of pointed tweezers comes in handy. A cotton Q-tip swab dipped in an insecticide is good for spot application.

Do not use any of your soils or mediums more than once. They may be carriers of bugs, fungus or disease. Soil that is used is just that, used. It will not be as good as new, fresh soil.

One of the best lines of defense is climate control. If you are keeping your humidity down with the use of exhaust fans and oscillating fans, bugs will find it difficult to maintain themselves in the blowing breeze. The moving air dries up excess water and helps to keep fungus, mold and mildew at a minimum. You must be creative with your exhaust systems and the removal of humidity, especially if you are growing in a tightly enclosed area, or a smaller area such as a walk-in closet.

Removing Bugs

There are a number of pests that are common to indoor marijuana. Before I list them, you must read the following information about using insecticides. If you do plan on growing, you will end up with an insect problem sooner or later, and at some point you will have to handle these poisonous substances.

There are other methods for removing bugs—if you have enough time on your hands, you can remove them manually or with suction devices (a household vacuum cleaner can come in handy here), but I have found the use of pyrethrum insecticides to be the safest and most effective way of controlling common grow-room pests.

A Few Words About Insecticides

Insecticides are dangerous. You should always wear protective clothing, especially rubber gloves and an apron (or even an entire rubber suit if you're the paranoid type), whenever you are handling them. When using sprayers be sure to stand downwind (or "downfan") from the spray. Always turn your exhaust system up to full power when using insecticides. Always wear the best protective breathing apparatus you can get.

I suggest that you give your plants a thorough rinsing with fresh water within 24 hours of each application. Carefully follow all the instructions on the label of whatever insecticide you purchase. Be sure to use only the standard solutions for whatever formulas are listed.

I try to use organic insecticides whenever possible. Pyrethrum is one of the best, safest and most effective natural insecticides. It comes in a concentrated form and is derived from the pyrethrum plant, which is a species of chrysanthemum (a well-known flower).

I also like to use Safer's brand insecticides—one of the safest and most effective. The company makes a few different types, including an insecticide soap.

While I do recommend the use of some chemical insecticides, please remember that these should be used only when all other methods have failed. Always handle chemical insecticides with care. Read all the instructions and warnings on the containers. Do not use them before the recommended time listed in the directions for any flowering plants before harvest. Finally, be sure to carefully dispose of the containers they come in.

Do not mix insecticides with fertilizers, fungicides or anything else. You should use tepid water when mixing insecticides. Spraying in the morning (or the early part of the indoor light cycle), is best because the spray will have the day to dry.

You should make sure that your plants are watered before you spray or fog them. The insecticides are strong and your plants will need the moisture in their systems.

A hand pump-sprayer, like the ones that come with plastic bottles of window cleaner, or a pressurized sprayer with a wand attachment are excellent for applying pesticides. Always use a separate sprayer for washing the plants with water.

Use a hand pump-sprayer with a fine-mist setting to wash the plants with water, and start at the top, spraying thoroughly both sides (top and bottom) of all leaves. Once you've finished, give the plants a medium watering. This will disperse any insecticide evenly through the soil. If you have used the proper concentrations for the pesticides, this won't harm the soil or roots.

If you don't want the rinse water to fall into the plants' soil, place them on their sides against a suitably-sized plastic sheet while rinsing.

If you disapprove of the use of any pesticides at all, there are alternatives, although I have found they don't always work—especially on serious bug infestations. Garlic has been known to repel insects. A few cloves or a bunch of garlic planted around the base of your mammas could not hurt and might help to keep them free of bugs.

Another method for preventing bugs is to give your plants a "soap wash." One tablespoon of Ivory soap added to a gallon of water, when applied to plants, will adhere to bugs' bodies and dry them up. Apply the soap liberally to the tops and undersides of leaves and at the junctions of stems, or simply dip the whole plant into the wash.

Here's an organic recipe that has reportedly been effective for removing whiteflies and aphids: add one tablespoon of dishwashing detergent to one cup of vegetable oil (peanut, safflower, corn, soybean or sunflower), shake well, and mix one or two tablespoons with a cup of water. Spray the mixture directly onto the insects and check the plants at least every week, continuing to spray as needed.

When you are purchasing seasonal items such as insecticides try to shop a season ahead. You may find that a lot of items that are used more in the summer are hard to find in the winter. Some places don't sell insecticides in the winter. You should obtain, if possible, all your gardening materials ahead of time unless you know where they may be easily purchased all year round.

A HAND-HELD LENS OR MAGNIFYING GLASS WILL HELP YOU SPOT BUGS BEFORE THEY BECOME A PROBLEM. YOU SHOULD CHECK THE PLANTS OFTEN, BECAUSE BY THE TIME LEAVES SHOW SPOTS, DISCOLORATION, AND OTHER SIGNS OF BUG INFESTATION, IT IS MORE DIFFICULT TO GET RID OF THEM.

Spider Mites

Most of the crops that I have seen have had a run-in with spider mites at one time or another, and chances are that you will run into them yourself. Spider mites are the hardest to control and eradicate. They are very small (1/100th to 1/16th of an inch), and resemble a spider or a crab. (Webster's Dictionary describes the mite as an arachnid.) They're so tiny you usually don't spot them until they have established a foothold. This is one important reason to examine your plants on a regular basis with a powerful magnifying glass.

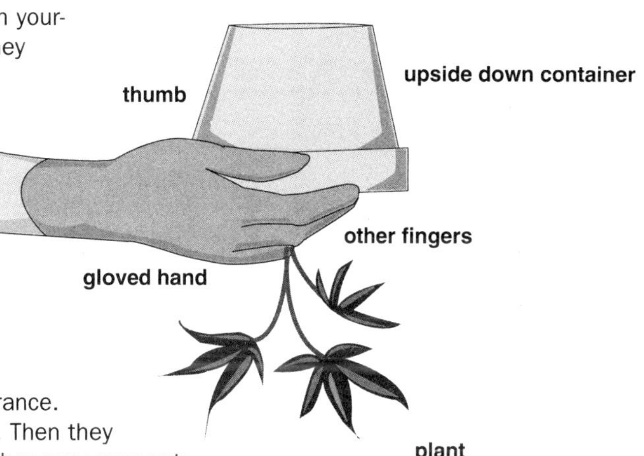

THIS IS HOW YOU HOLD A PLANT FOR THE PLANT-DIP.

You usually spot the "sign" first. You will notice that the top of one of the food leaves seems to have some tiny yellowish spots on it. These spots might be so small they'll look like tiny speckles. This is the clue to infestation. Remove the food leaf from the plant and examine the underside of the leaf.

Young spider mites have a yellowish or translucent appearance. (That is, until they begin to suck the juice out of your poor plant. Then they turn a pleasant green.) Adult spider mites are different colors. They may appear to be light brown, tan, black or colored and partially transparent. Some may look white or have two spots on them. False spider mites are red. You may also notice a stringy white substance on the underside of the leaf. This is a web. You might also see clusters of small white spots. These are usually the eggs. Mites often suck the juice from under the leaf and you may notice the damage more easily. You might also see some tiny black dots. You know what that is, don't you? Defecation.

One of the first things you should do is drop your temperature to around 60 degrees (Fahrenheit). The spider mites like temperatures above 70.

You may only have a local infestation, so isolate the plants that are infected from the uninfected ones. You may dip a Q-tip cotton swab in an organic pyrethrum insecticide, standard strength, and swab the entire area around the infestation. Make sure to get totally inside the crevices made at the nodes, above and below the trouble area.

Another method to eradicate larger infestations is the entire "plant dip." First, get a pair of rubber gloves and a plastic apron (always be careful when working with insectides). Then fill a suitably-sized container with the recommended amount of organic pyrethrum insecticide. (Follow the directions on the label for the correct amount to use for your situation.) On top of the soil at the base of the plant stem, position your fingers to surround the stem as you place your hand flat on the soil. Then dip the entire plant down to the base of the stem into the mixture, being careful not to get any insecticide on your hands. (If you happen to get the insecticide on your skin, follow the directions on the label). This method will hold the plant in the container as you turn it upside down and dip it in the solution. Shake the plant around vigorously in the solution for about 10 or 15 seconds, swirling around and up and down.

After immersing the entire plant in the pyrethrum "bath," take it out of the solution and let it drip dry for a few minutes, shaking it slightly to remove excess liquid. If you have the room, put a plastic cloth on the floor so the containers don't drip the solution on the floor after they are removed. If you direct your shaking downward you will get less on yourself. When you turn the plant rightside up, some of the liquid will drip on the soil. This won't permanently damage your plant—the pyrethrum becomes inert and inactive after just a few hours. Water your plant to help wash the solution into the soil. This will get any bugs that might be lurking there. The next day, rinse your plant thoroughly with water.

If your plant is under a foot tall, you should use a container slightly deeper than a foot. Using the above method, a standard 5-gallon bucket usually works for most plants. Small clones might only need a quart-sized container. I don't use the "plant dip" for large mammas, but you could try it if everything else fails. If so, you'll probably want to buy a large plastic garbage can.

Another solution is to buy an aerosol pyrethrum spray and discharge it into the area infected with the mites. When using these sprays, be sure that the freezing ingredients, emitted directly from the nozzle, don't fall directly on any vegetation. Keep the can a few feet away from your plants when you set it off. These sprays are very thorough and will penetrate into all the crevices where spider mites might dwell. You should repeat the process in 7 to 10 days (the time it takes the eggs to hatch), just to make sure that you have killed all the mites. Some eggs might have survived and hatched. If so, the second application will get them. If you want to be dead certain that you've removed all traces of spider mites, give the plants a third application.

The clone or plant dipped into the pyrethrum or sprayed with the aerosol will contain no traces of the insecticide, and these are very effective ways of administering the pyrethrum. It is not as drastic as it might sound (chemical insecticides are a much more harmful and desperate solution), but it is cumbersome and time-consuming.

The only time I resorted to these types of bug-control methods (bombing and plant dips), is when I was faced with a severe mite problem that had spread to the clones, then the preflowers, and then to the flowers. I destroyed the mammas, then dipped the clones and preflowers. I aerosol-bombed the bloomers that were up to 60 days old; those that were in the last thirty days of blooming were harvested early. That crop had a blooming time of 90 days. Twelve days later I sprayed the remaining plants and the entire room with pyrethrum. The problem was solved.

Whiteflies

The whitefly is probably the second most common bug you will have to contend with. Because most of them have wings, they can spread faster than spider mites. The "sign" of whitefly infestation is similar to that of spider mites. You may notice some spots on the lower leaves. Actually, you'll more likely notice the moth-like 1/16th" white adult quickly flutter from one plant to another.

If you see a whitefly larvae you might think it's a mite. Closer examination of the undersides of the leaves may indicate a whitefly infestation. If you don't see webbing or black defecation it is probably a whitefly. Another indicator will be the small honey-colored droplets secreted by whiteflies.

You can purchase yellow whitefly traps that are similar to flypaper at most hardware stores and nursery shops. Hung above the plants, their yellow color attracts the whiteflies, who get stuck in the sticky trap. They are effective but won't eradicate the problem, just help to control it.

If you find a serious infestation, I suggest the use of pyrethrum aerosol—three applications 7 to 10 days apart, as with the spider mite situation. (Do not use pyrethrum aerosol, or any insecticide, on flowers 30 days or less prior to harvest.) If that doesn't work, consider the use of Malathion or Diazinon—again, only as a last resort. These are used in a standard mixture that is thoroughly sprayed on the plants—apply three applications every 7 to 10 days. The Malathion or Diazinon should be used only on plants that are in the vegetative stage and should never be used on any flowers.

THIS SMALL "MAMMA" SHOULD HAVE HER LOWER, INNER BRANCHES TRIMMED. INSECTS MAY HIDE AND GET A FOOTHOLD THERE. PRUNING LOWER LEAVES WILL ALSO IMPROVE PLANT GROWTH IN THE REMAINING BRANCHES.

Aphids

Aphids are about as big as the head of a pin. They are easier to spot than spider mites—you can see them moving around on your plant without a magnifying glass. They may be yellow, green or black, and, like spider mites, excrete a honey-colored droplet. They are usually found on the growing terminals.

Again I suggest the standard use of the pyrethrum aerosol, 3 applications every 7 to 10 days. On plants that will be harvested within 30 days, you may consider vacuuming and then hand-picking any bugs that are left.

Mealy Bugs

Mealy bugs are easy to spot. They are about 1/16 to 1/4" long, have a waxy white color and give off honey-colored secretions. Usually found congregated around the nodes and along the stem, they are slow-moving and fairly easy to control. Use a spray on the infected area, and then lightly spray the entire plant. Apply three times every 7 to 10 days.

Predator Mites

Some people use predatory insects, such as ladybugs, lacewings or predator mite species, to control spider mites, whiteflies and other pests. I can't recommend them as a solution as they are time-consuming, expensive and rarely 100% effective, but most of all, they are difficult to purchase unless you resort to mail-order.

If you decide to use them (anyone who chooses to grow marijuana with strict organic guidelines will start with predators for pest control), it's best if you can purchase them directly from a shop and don't have to resort to mail-order. However, it is usually difficult to find a local store that keeps these in stock. (If you must resort to mail-order, a few sources are Nature's Control in Medford, OR, and Rincon-Vitova in Oakview, CA. The drawbacks are that many of the bugs can die during shipping unless you pick them up immediately on delivery, and of course there are always security concerns whenever you purchase anything through the mail.) I have found ladybugs at the local nursery, but their availability is seasonal.

If you are determined to grow as organically as possible, you will have to weigh your reasons against those in favor of faster and more effective ways to control pests. You must rely on the predators to eat every last mite and egg. Once the supply of food (in this case the pests), is eaten, the predators starve to death—their reward for their service to you. Worst of all, if they don't eat all the spider mite eggs the latter will hatch, and the problem will start all over again.

There are other problems in using predatory insects in an indoor garden. Predators that can fly, such as ladybugs, will get "zapped" when they fly into a metal halide or other HID light. Predator mites have certain requirements—and thrive in specific climates which you will need to ascertain. Also, remember that any insecticides you are using will kill off your predators as well.

The Ultimate Weapon

If any of the above-mentioned processes fail to get rid of your mite problem, there is one "ultimate weapon" we suggest: the use of Sevin or Malathion. Use this only if all of your other efforts fail. The Sevin or Malathion should be mixed in a standard solution. To this you add 8 drops of horticultural petroleum oil per gallon of solution. This will be applied in a thorough spraying every 7 to 10 days for three applications. You should only use this in the vegetative stage of the plant life. If your plants are in the flowering stage I suggest the use of the pyrethrum aerosol or the soap-based alternatives mentioned earlier. Do not use anything on your flowers less than 30 days prior to harvest.

"MARIJUANA: ASSASSIN OF YOUTH"

by Harry J. Anslinger

REEFER

MACNEILL

SECURITY

Although I have mentioned some security concerns throughout the book, I thought that a chapter devoted to security would help.

Growing marijuana is now one of the most illegal activities you can be involved in. Getting caught can result in a long prison term. Under certain circumstances and in some parts of the country, life imprisonment or even the death penalty can be called for. Ironically, this is also why growing marijuana can be so profitable.

Snitches

Many people are under the impression that helicopters using infrared detectors or utility companies noticing excessive electrical usage are the most common ways through which marijuana growers are caught. However, most of the time growers have been turned in by informants. Most often, they are former friends or associates.

While reading this book, you've probably noticed that growing marijuana takes a lot of time and effort. Obviously, if you team up with other people it will reduce your responsibility for tending the crops every day. Just remember that every other person who knows about your activity adds to the risk of getting caught.

You never know who a snitch could turn out to be. In many parts of the country, the rewards offered for turning over marijuana growers are so substantial that you should consider anyone you know, or meet, as a potential informant. Of course, you should never brag about your garden, nor sell your product to anyone you don't know. (If a friend, even someone you know and trust, wants to introduce you to a stranger who makes an offer that's so good it's hard to believe, decline and let your "friend" make the big sale without your help. This is the most common setup—the one that attempts to play on your greed.)

Never show or give large, unmanicured buds, abundant supply of leaf or other evidence of an indoor grow operation to people who don't know what you are up to. Likewise, if you are able to make some side money through your efforts, don't spend it on obvious signs of wealth: gold chains, a big car, a big TV or stereo set, etc.

Location

Certain parts of the country have harsher laws than others. Laws have been changing too often for us to attempt to list them here. Find out what the penalties for cultivation are in your state. You can call the government from a pay phone if you want to be very careful, but find out what they are before you start anything. You should think hard about the risks you face if you are growing in a state with harsh laws. And, if you are successful at growing, you should try to use some of that money to help change the laws.

Make sure your garden is as secure as possible. No sounds, smells, lights or plants should be visible from outside the location. You should walk around the property and check it thoroughly as often as possible—no less than once a week.

Lawyers

You should make every effort to hire one before you start a grow room. To find one in your area, you can contact NORML (1-900-97NORML or 1-900-976-6765). They offer an excellent legal referral service that can locate lawyers in your jurisdiction.

Of course, you won't tell the lawyer why you want to talk to him (or her). Say you're thinking of writing up a will, or need help on purchasing real estate, when you contact the law office. If you can, set up a short consultation to get a feel for what he can offer, and take a look at how they run their business. Does he seem organized? Does he seem trustworthy?

Once you choose a lawyer, keep the phone number on your person at all times or memorize it. If something goes wrong, it will come in handy.

LEFT: THIS PROPAGANDA ILLUSTRATION FROM THE 1930S IS A PRIME EXAMPLE OF THE ANTI-MARIJUANA HYSTERIA THAT LED TO ITS PROHIBITION. SADLY, THE SAME KIND OF HYSTERIA IS BEING SPREAD BY POLITICIANS AND ANTI-DRUG WARRIORS TODAY.

How To Avoid Being Noticed

You can't become invisible, but you should avoid drawing attention to yourself, your car or your house. For instance:

1. Keep your car neat. Don't have any smoking materials in it (roaches, pipes, bongs, or even rolling papers).
2. Your house and its surroundings should fit into the neighborhood. Keep the lawn mowed, keep the house painted, and make sure there are no violations that would enable the police to stop by for an inspection (i.e., trash or litter, wild parties).
3. Of course, do not wear pot-leaf t-shirts in public.

If You're Being Watched

If someone does turn your name in as a possible suspect, or if the police "just want to talk" to you, follow some simple rules:

1. Don't ever talk to the police without having a lawyer present.
2. Tell your lawyer about any kind of harassment or suspicion by the police.
3. Make sure you carry a valid driver's license, or I.D., and that your car has the proper, updated registration and is legal and insured.

In Case Of A Bust

If the worst happens, follow a few basic guidelines:

1. Don't offer resistance, and don't get angry and shout or throw insults, even if they try to egg you on. Acting in this way can get you in much more trouble down the road, if and when you go to trial and your behavior is described during testimony.
2. Don't talk about the (alleged) offense, or anything regarding it. Silence is golden. Make no statements—true or false. Keep your mouth shut.
3. Once you have the Miranda rights read to you, you will have the right to call an attorney. Don't admit to anything or even talk about the offense over the phone in the police station, even if you think you can't be overheard. And don't bring anyone else's name into it.
4. Don't become a snitch, no matter what the offer. If your lawyer pressures you into doing it, fire him and hire one who will look after your needs. If everyone involved keeps quiet, it could be very difficult for the government to prove anything.

Evidence

The garbage you place outside your home can be used in court as evidence that a crime has taken place. The police can pick it up, examine it, and if it contains incriminating evidence, bust you for it. And they don't need a search warrant to do so. They can simply ask the garbage collector to cooperate and turn over your garbage. If there is any evidence of marijuana use or cultivation inside (even rolling papers, a roach or seeds), the police can get a search warrant based on that evidence. So be careful of what you're throwing away. You might want to keep a separate garbage can for anything incriminating and carry that to a remote dumpster.

Electric bills can also be used by police to show evidence of marijuana cultivation. Although a bust or warrant is unlikely to result from that alone, almost anything else could be used to order a search. Utility companies have been cooperating with the police in helping to locate marijuana-growing operations (as have UPS offices).

Top Ten Ways to Get Arrested for Indoor Cultivation

1. Once you complete your first harvest, throw a party and share your good fortune with all of your friends.

2. Sell some of your excess crop to someone you don't know.

3. Get in a big fight with your girlfriend, boyfriend, partner or relative. Make sure the fight is nasty enough that they will want to turn you over to the police to get revenge.

4. Go to a bar and get drunk and brag about your grow room to someone you meet for the first time.

5. Order your grow lights through the mail (and use your credit card).

6. Buy your light system at a store that specializes in indoor grow equipment. Remember to drive your own car and to pay with a credit card.

7. Grow in a densely-populated area, cover all the windows with black plastic (making obvious that something criminal is going on inside), and act furtively when neighbors approach you.

8. Cover your investment first, instead of your ass. Don't break up the grow room at the first signal of potential trouble—hope that the whole thing blows over.

9. Don't bother to cover your tracks—throw away all your old potting-soil bags and used fertilizer containers in the garbage. Or better yet, just leave them in the backyard.

10. Buy your supplies from the same store, and ask the salespeople suspicious questions about your "tomato crop." Wink when you say "tomato."

Sea Of Green

SECTION 2

THE SEED

The selection of the seed is one of the most important decisions you will make when you decide to grow. This is because the act of growing marijuana can be boiled down to two things: 1. Following some simple rules; 2. Plant genetics. The average seed will produce a plant similar or identical to its parent. Therefore if you take any given seed and manipulate its environment in the right way, you will get a plant similar to the parent plant.

Finding good seed stock

The simplest way to find good seed stock is to save seeds from any good smoke you come across. If you live in an area where your local supplier is conversant with different marijuana seed strains and has access to them, you might even be able to procure the seeds this way.

There are many seed companies (also called seed banks) that will mail them to the United States. *Cannabis Canada* (a bimonthly publication available on many US newsstands) often lists some of these seed companies. Many others can be found by searching the Internet.

NOTE: It is illegal to import cannabis seeds into the United States under any circumstances. Also, not all seed companies are legitimate. Some will pocket the cash you mail. (Of course, you would have to be completely insane to send one of these outfits credit-card information or your home address.) Seed companies that sell to the United States have been closed down by the Drug Enforcement Administration and customer lists confiscated. Some can even be secret fronts for DEA “sting” operations. We strongly suggest that anyone considering growing marijuana find sources for seeds outside of these mail-order companies, as convenient as they might seem.

The best way to find the world’s best seed stock is to travel to Amsterdam, where seeds are sold commercially through grow stores and magazines. Bringing them back is a risky proposition, unless you live in a country where possession of cannabis seeds is legal. They can be detected when sent through the mail even if they are packaged securely. Although there is not a strong, telltale odor from seeds as there is from buds, sometimes US Customs officials will randomly search people. Since Amsterdam’s reputation as a haven for marijuana consumers and growers has grown, there is often increased security on return flights from Holland.

As of this writing, there are also many businesses in Canada that sell cannabis seeds over the counter. There is no way to predict how long this situation will last. This could be the beginning of marijuana legalization in Canada, or the seed shops could all be closed down by the time this book is in print. We have decided against printing any names or addresses in this book, as this attention could encourage the US government to close them down.

Once an American citizen purchases marijuana seeds from a foreign establishment, there are ways to minimize the risks in carrying back or mailing the seeds, but it would take another book to provide the details. A drastic option that some marijuana growers have chosen to take is to change their citizenship and move to Canada, Holland, Germany, or any other of the growing number of countries that are becoming tolerant of marijuana use.

Selecting the Seed

Seeds come in a variety of sizes and colors. They range from about 1/10” to 1/4” in width. The color may range from light-brown to almost gray to dark-brown, almost black. They may have “tiger stripes” or “lightning stripes” on them, or irregular, different-colored lines. If a seed has a light-green or white color, it is usually immature. When the seed is covered with a waxy sheath, this outer coating gives a healthy seed a waxy, live look.

I like to make sure that, aside from having good genes from good parents, my seeds pass a physical examination prior to germination. I use a magnifying glass to examine each seed, making sure there are no cracks or imperfections in any of them. Under a magnifying glass the best seeds seem to stand out.

Preparing for Germination

Once you are satisfied that you have made your best selection of seeds, you will want to germinate them. This process will be the same regardless of quantity.

Here we will demonstrate germination in small peat-moss squares and our standard soil mixture. If you wish to use this method, then by all means do so. We also, however, encourage you to experiment with different ways of doing the same thing. If we call for small peat-moss cups and you can't afford or find them, then think of some alternative devices to use, such as a Dixie cup or the clean bottom of a used milk carton.

For example, one very popular method used to germinate seeds is the "paper-towel method." You simply place the seeds within layers of paper towels, place them on a dish or saucer, and make sure to keep the paper towels moist at all times. After several days the seeds will sprout, and once they have grown an inch or two long they can be transplanted into soil-filled containers.

OBTAINING GOOD SEED STOCK CAN BE THE MOST DIFFICULT PART OF GROWING GOOD MARIJUANA. ONE EASY WAY IS TO REMOVE THE SEEDS FROM ANY GOOD MARIJUANA YOU BUY TO SMOKE. COLLECT ALL THE SEEDS, THEN SELECT THE BEST FOR GERMINATION. REMEMBER: THE BEST SEEDS WILL PRODUCE THE BEST SMOKE.

Popular Seed Varieties

The two species of marijuana that are grown for recreational use are Cannabis *sativa* and Cannabis *indica*. *Sativa* plants tend to grow tall and produce small yields, with users experiencing a spacy, even energetic high. *Indica* plants are usually shorter than *sativas* but fuller but yield more buds, and users experience a heavier, more narcotic buzz. Most varieties are hybrids of *sativa* and *indica* and exhibit characteristics of both. Nowadays, few pure strains of either are commercially available. The pure *indica* breeds tend to be popular with indoor growers because of their large yields. Most popular varieties of marijuana have been developed in Holland, where cannabis seeds are sold over the counter. Afghani plants are usually powerful *indica* varieties, while Thai or Mexican breeds are usually pure *sativas*.

The Sensi Seed Bank is the most famous commercial producer of cannabis seeds. They have trademarked their most popular varieties, which have become as famous to modern connoisseurs as Panama Red and Acapulco Gold were to smokers in the 1960s. As you can see, the flowering times and yields differ with each breed.

Northern Lights #5 X Haze
mostly *sativa* hybrid

Haze is a very powerful *sativa* hybrid (from Mexican and Colombian breeds with traces of South Indian and Thai) that was developed in the late 1980s. It was difficult to grow indoors, and its yield was poor, but it blended well with other strains. Northern Lights is a pure *indica* that features dense, full buds and is a favorite of indoor growers. The resulting hybrid has won many awards, including the prestigious 1994 Cannabis Cup.
Flowering: 65-75 days
Height: 150-180 centimeters
Yield: up to 150 grams

Big Bud
mostly *indica* hybrid

One of the most popular Sensi Seed Bank varieties, Big Bud promises such big yields that the Sensi Seed Bank warns growers: "It is advisable to tie up the bottom branches, as they have a tendency to break due to their excessive weight."
Flowering: 50-65 days
Height: 110-150 centimeters
Yield: up to 150 grams

Jack Herer
sativa/indica hybrid

This runaway winner of the 1996 Cannabis Cup combines "three of the strongest varieties known to man." Its pedigree details are so secret that details of whether it is mostly *sativa* or *indica* are unknown.
Flowering: 50-70 days
Height: 150-180 centimeters
Yield: up to 125 grams

Skunk #1
mostly *sativa* hybrid

One of the most famous cannabis strains in the world, Skunk #1 was the winner of the first-ever Cannabis Cup in 1988. A Thai/Mexican/Afghani hybrid, it is a favorite of greenhouse growers because of its consistency and large buds.
Flowering: 45-50 days
Height: 120-150 centimeters
Yield: up to 100 grams

Afghani #1
pure *indica*

A typical *indica* breed, these plants feature big, dark leaves, a strong aroma, sturdy stems and a high yield.
Flowering: 45 days
Height: 100-130 centimeters
Yield: up to 125 grams

Hawaiian Indica
pure *indica*

A Hawaiian crossed with Northern Lights that has a long flowering period.
Flowering: 60-65 days
Height: 120-150 centimeters
Yield: up to 125 grams

Super Skunk
mostly *indica*

This variety was developed by crossing Skunk with the original Afghani strains it was bred from. It has become more popular than Skunk #1 with many smokers and growers.
Flowering: 45-50 days
Height: 120-150 centimeters
Yield: up to 125 grams

GERMINATION

Our standard method is to germinate in soil. First we put together a standard soil mixture, made of easy-to-obtain ingredients. It's a simple, organic natural medium: clean, easy to work with and conducive to the growing process. I have found that soil-type environments are more forgiving to the learning process than other growing media.

The Soil Mixture

The soil mixture we have had the most success with is 1/2 potting soil and 1/2 coarse horticultural perlite with approximately 1/24 pasteurized cow manure. We have been known to use up to 1/3 cow manure. After a while you may want to experiment with this factor. For the setup shown in these photographs, we used approximately 3 gallons potting soil and 3 gallons perlite with one quart of cow manure and two heaping tablespoons of horticultural hydrated lime. As this is a more or less manmade soil, we find it is helpful to add the organic manure. It is nutritious and the fiber helps texture the soil. The lime is hydrated and quick-releasing. It will help to balance the pH and add useful calcium (Ca) and magnesium (Mg) to the soil.

You should use the best potting soil you can find. I like Peter's because it is usually clean—free of bugs and fungi. If you are not sure about the cleanliness of your soil, moisten it lightly, spread it a few inches deep on a tray and place it in a preheated oven for 45 minutes to an hour at 160-170°F. This "cooking" process will kill most bugs or fungi that may be lurking.

Mix the potting soil, perlite and cow manure thoroughly. You will want to use a proper breathing device (a face mask) when mixing perlite. If mixing indoors, be sure to have an exhaust fan blowing across your work area and out an open window. It is very unhealthy to breathe perlite, which is bad for your lungs.

Soil Containers

Once you have mixed your standard soil mixture, place it into suitable containers. I prefer to use either small peat cups or small plastic containers, such as the ones you see in the photographs. Whatever container I use, and regardless of quantity, I like to place them in these small plastic trays. They are useful for a number of reasons. They contain a specific number of plants, which tend to separate themselves from those in the other trays. This way, if you have a problem with the plants in one tray, it usually stays in that tray. Also, if you over-water the tray, the excess water can simply be poured out. The trays also facilitate the easy movement of the seedlings if you wish to inspect or work with them.

The other type of container I like to germinate seeds in is the root cube. These cubes hold water very well, and it is difficult to accidentally over-water when using them. The cubes come in slabs that fit into the plastic trays. They are also very porous and can hold lots of water. It is very easy and convenient to put the felt root-cube slabs into the plastic trays and add about a gallon of water. If you remove one of the corner cubes from the slab, it will help you to determine more accurately the status of the water in the tray. The root slab should be completely saturated. (Directly after watering the root cubes, there may be some standing water. If there is too much, pour it out. Leaving a small amount of standing water, however, will not harm the plants.) Sometimes root cubes that have nutrients already prepared specifically for seedlings may be purchased.

Whether you are using peat cups, small plastic cups or root cubes, the process will be the same. Always use tepid water (warm, not hot).

Let's start with the root cubes. Using a standard, non-nutrient slab (placed in a plastic tray), saturate the root-cube slab with tepid water. Then take the seeds and place one into each cube. Make sure that the seed goes at least halfway down into the prepunched hole of the cube. Then take the recommended amount of B1 (a nutrient useful for the rooting process found in commercial solutions such as Up-Start, SuperThrive, Hormex, and others) and give your root-cube slab another watering. Be sure to place a small amount of water on each individual cube.

If you are planting your seeds into soil, do basically the same thing. Take a gallon of water and saturate your containers of soil in the trays. Whether you are using peat cups or plastic cups, pour out any excess water. Take a pointed object, such as a pencil, and make a small hole approximately 1/2" deep in the soil in the center of the container. Then place one seed into each hole, making sure the seed goes most of the way down. Cover the seed by simply pressing the soil over the top of the hole with your finger. Then water lightly with your B1 or Up-Start. I like to water the soil or the root cubes first with regular water to saturate the medium, then use the nutrients on the second watering.

The trays are then covered using tray-type tops; a simple plastic-wrap cover will do. The cover helps to hold in moisture and create humidity. If you are working in a room with a lot of humidity, it will increase the likelihood that molds will start growing on your containers or soil, so you will not want to use the coverings.

You will now place your planted seeds in a warm (80-90°F), dark environment. I usually place mine in the cloning rack with the lights off. This gives me total control over their environment. At first, check your seeds a couple of times a day. Make sure that your soil remains damp but not saturated. This can be managed simply by using small amounts when you water, rather than watering a lot each time. Remember at all times to pour out any excess water from your trays. Make sure the exhaust-fan part of your cloning area is turned on and include any heating or cooling systems.

Your project has officially started.

When The Seeds Sprout

A seed does not need light to germinate. As long as it is given the proper environmental conditions of moisture and temperature, a viable seed will germinate. The root of the seed aims itself downward, following gravity. The hypocotyl, or grow tip of the new plantlet, aims upward, driven by cellular growth. Reaching for the light, the first two rounded leaves, the cotyledons, soon appear. The single embryonic root soon forms lateral rootlets. These tiny rootlets serve a number of functions. They absorb nutrients and water from the soil, and as they grow, the plant grows. You must make sure that these rootlets are not damaged whenever a transplanting is done. They may be damaged by exposure to light, air or rough treatment.

After three to 10 days the seeds will begin to open. You should remove any covers on the trays or on individual containers immediately upon an indication of germination (root appears from seed). Once I have noticed a few sets of cotyledons beginning to appear, I turn on my lights and start the seedlings on an 18-hour-a-day light schedule. I usually like to start the 40-watt fluorescent tubes about 6" to 8" above the tops of the sprouts. About a week after all the seeds have sprouted, I lower the lights so that the bottom of the bulb is almost touching the top of the plant. Try 3" away from the top for a day. If it doesn't stress the plant, lower the light by half (1 1/2"). That should be close enough.

Once the lights are turned on, you may notice that the soil medium you are using dries out more quickly and may require more frequent watering. If you are germinating your seeds in soil, you may notice that each individual container will dry out at the same time as all the other containers in a certain tray. However, you will also notice that some containers seem to dry out sooner or later than others. For this reason you must pay close attention to each individual container. You may still water the whole tray at one time; just make sure some containers get a little more water and some get a little less, depending on your careful observations.

Once your seedlings have been up for a few days, you may start watering them less. Let the top inch of their container dry out while the lower few inches remain damp. This helps the young plant breathe.

As the seedlings begin to grow you will need to raise the light fixtures, keeping them just above the point where they might burn. I have found that about 1" to 2" is sufficient. Feel free to experiment. After germination we like to keep the average temperature of the room around 75 to 80°F.

The humidity of the area may be kept at the proper level by use of the exhaust-fan system. We like to keep the humidity between 50 and 70%; the closer to 50%, the better.

As The Seedlings Grow

THE SMALL SEEDLINGS IN THE 2 1/2" PEAT MOSS SQUARES ARE TRANSPLANTED INTO LARGER, 5 1/4" PLASTIC CONTAINERS. KEEPING THE CONTAINERS ORGANIZED IN TRAYS WILL HELP IN WATERING.

Once your cotyledons appear, they will open and the root will anchor itself firmly into the soil. Once this happens, more leaves will begin to sprout from the center of the growing terminal. These secondary leaves will not be rounded, as were the first cotyledons. They will be serrated and have a pointed tip. At first, they are single-bladed, but will soon be followed by three-fingered, then five-fingered leaves, etc. As the seedlings grow, their root systems continue to branch out as do their stems and leaves.

The stem carries water and nutrients up the plant, using some on the way and distributing the rest to the other functions of the seedling, such as creating new foliage. It is a good idea to have an oscillating fan on your seedlings, as the blowing fan takes the place of the wind they would be exposed to in nature. The movement of the plant caused by the moving air stimulates cellulose growth in the stem and gives the plant rigidity and strength to stand and hold its own weight without falling over.

It is a good idea to spray your leaves once a week or so with regular water, using a fine mist from a spray bottle. This helps keep your plants clean, so they will breathe better and be better able to engage in photosynthesis. Cleaning the plant clears the tiny stomata on the underside of the leaves, which assist photosynthesis by breathing in air.

Once the seedlings begin to leave the kernel of the seed, they can begin to utilize light. I like to keep them under the fluorescent grow tubes for about 30 days after germination. It is around that time that I transplant them into 5 1/4" squares. If you want to keep them under a metal-halide lamp from the time they germinate, be sure to start your light at least 24" from the tops of the fragile young seedlings so that they do not burn. They should receive 18 hours a day of continuous light.

Once the seeds germinate, they do not need the high temperature we suggested for germination, 80° to 90°F. They should be placed in a temperature more fitting for the vegetative state: 75° to 80°F.

You will usually not have to fertilize the seedlings before 30 days. This is because there already are nutrients in the standard soil mixture: the Peter's potting soil, the cow manure and the B1. I usually start the plants on a fertilizing schedule after they have been transplanted into the 5 1/4" squares. However, if the seedlings should appear to need a fertilization during these 30 days, then do so. If the lower leaves begin to yellow, I suggest you start them with a 1/2 or 1/4-strength regimen.

Seedlings need fresh air. Be sure to keep your air circulation going from this time on.

Transplanting The Seedlings

After your plants have grown for about three or four weeks, they will have developed some foliage and a fair number of roots. Then they will be ready to transplant into larger 5 1/4" square containers.

It is at this time that I like to start the plants on a regular feeding of SuperThrive. Simply follow the instructions on the container. Use each time you employ a standard fertilizer.

If my seedlings were started in peat-moss cups, I hold the cup upside down, shake gently and remove the plant. If the roots have grown into the peat-moss cup, you should simply plant the entire cup into the 5 1/4" container. If you started your seedlings in plastic containers, you will find that simply inverting the container and giving it a sharp shake will dislodge the plant, roots and all.

To transplant the seedlings into the 5 1/4" square containers, fill the container almost full with the standard soil mixture. Moisten the soil with regular water, then make a depression large enough to receive the transplant. Place the transplant into the depression and press the soil around the base of the stem. Never bury the stem deeper than it originally was. Water with the standard amount of transplanting aid (B1).

If you germinated your seeds in root cubes, you will follow a similar process. About a week or 10 days after the seeds germinate, you will notice that they have developed roots which are beginning to grow through the cubes. The plant may then be separated from the cube with a sharp object such as a knife. (Obviously, you won't cut the plant, only the cube, with the knife.) You should then place the plant into a peat-moss cup filled with the standard soil mixture which has been moistened with regular water. After transplanting they may be lightly watered with the standard transplanting aid. Once they are about four weeks old, they may again be transplanted into the 5 1/4" squares, using the standard transplanting method.

When your seedlings are about five to six weeks old they will have reached a height of 12" to 14", and will have developed some nice foliage and six or seven separate main nodes. They are now ready for our special process for determining the sex, or gender, of the plants.

The standard soil mixture, combined with the application of the B1 during transplanting and the recommended dosage of SuperThrive, usually contains enough nutrients to feed your plants up to this point in their lives. However, around the fifth or sixth week, they may begin to show some yellowing of the lower food leaves. If you see this happening at any point during this period, it is time to fertilize. If your plants are not showing any nutrient needs when they are five or six weeks old, you should nevertheless start them on their routine fertilization schedule.

Care And Feeding Of The Plants

These seedlings are large enough now to refer to as plants. Once you determine their sex, the females will be used as your "mammas." Therefore, you should start their routine fertilizing around the sixth week after germination (unless they show a need sooner). This should be a standard fertilization, according to the instructions on the container of whatever fertilizer you choose. I use a full-spectrum vegetable fertilizer, which has a total supply of primary nutrients and micronutrients. If you want to use a fertilizer such as fish emulsion or worm castings, feel free. Fertilizing plants is usually done once every two weeks, unless the plants are showing signs of needing it sooner. If they show signs of overfertilization, flush them immediately and transplant them into clean soil. Be sure to read the information in the earlier sections of the book to understand correct fertilization.

THIS 12-INCH SEEDLING IS READY TO HAVE ITS GENDER DETERMINED.

Plant Seedlings

Once your seedling has developed a reasonable number of roots and some nice foliage and has grown to the height of about 10 inches, we consider it a parent seedling. It will have anywhere from five to eight nodes and be mature enough to show gender, if the proper conditions are met.

The old standard method for determining the sex of marijuana is time-consuming and detrimental to your parent seedling. This is done by manipulating the photoperiod of your seedling.

Marijuana is photoperiodic, which means that as long as a plant is receiving 18 to 24 hours of daily light it will continue to grow in the vegetative state. If the light period is reduced to only 12 hours a day the plant will then enter the flowering stage and indicate its gender.

Using the old method of determining sex, you must germinate your seeds and grow them to a reasonable age and height under 18 or more hours of light per day. This means growing them for approximately three to four weeks or until they have reached the approximate height of 10 to 12 inches, then reducing the light schedule to 12 hours a day. After about three weeks the seedlings will begin to indicate gender. Once this is accomplished and all the females and males have been determined you must now return the light period of the females to the original 18 hours or so a day which returns them to the vegetative state. This wastes almost two months of your time and stresses your plants unduly.

Using our special process we are able to determine the sex of all your parent seedlings without reducing the light period in about three weeks. This saves you time, work, and effort while saving your parent seedlings from undue stress. Let's look at this method in a little more detail.

Making Cheap CO_2

One of the best ways to spur plant growth is to increase the amount of carbon dioxide (CO_2) the plants receive. Growers have done everything from letting their dog sleep in the growroom to setting up a natural-gas CO_2 generator.

The Baking-soda Method

Here is one method for setting up a low-maintenance, low-technology way to produce CO_2 on demand (originally published in the January 1989 issue of HIGH TIMES):

Mixing vinegar (dilute acetic acid) with a slurry of baking soda (sodium bicarbonate) is a fantastic low-technology way to produce CO_2 on demand. There are several advantages to this technique.

1) Waste products are simply disposed of down the toilet without hurting the environment.

2) There is no burning of hydrocarbons such as gas or oil, which produce pollution.

3) No heat is produced, so less has to be removed from the grow room.

4) This technique is more convenient than lugging big, heavy CO_2 cylinders.

5) Purchasing baking soda and vinegar at your local supermarket and transporting these items in grocery bags garners a lot less attention than buying CO_2 tanks.

6) You don't have to purchase an expensive gas regulator-metering device.

Producing CO_2 by fermenting sugar is interesting, but fermentation costs more than the vinegar/baking soda method and requires more maintenance.

I put 1/3 cup of baking soda in a 2.25 quart pitcher, and cover it with a minimal amount of water to make a slurry of baking soda. I built a little platform on the pitcher mouth which holds an 8-ounce cup of vinegar. The cup has a strip of tissue placed in the inside bottom which extends over the top and below the bottom, so that it acts as a siphon. It takes several hours to drain the cup, one drop every 15-30 seconds, into a pitcher. I add more vinegar to the cup as needed. When the pitcher is nearly full, I simply pour the contents down the toilet and refill the cup and pitcher.

The Fermentation Method

Max Yields offered this method of CO_2 production on his Web site column (**www.hightimes.com**). It will work as an alternative to CO_2 injection but will require sugar as well as yeast and water. The following is a recipe for creating CO_2 by fermentation:

You'll need a container, with a lid that can hold five gallons or more, and a 6' to 10' length of hose approximately one-half inch in diameter.

Cut a hole in the center of the lid large enough for the hose to fit into. Use a silicone-based sealant to seal one end of the hose to the lid. The whole setup should be airtight.

Place the container in the growroom and fill it with four gallons of water. Then boil one gallon of water on the stove and add 6 to 10 cups of sugar. Allow the water to boil again and make sure all the sugar has dissolved.

Carefully take the hot sugar water, mix it with the four gallons in the container, and add one packet of baker's yeast. Let stand for 15 minutes, then stir the mixture and put the lid on the container.

Run the other end of the hose into a glass of water. In a day or two the yeast will begin turning the sugar into alcohol, and CO_2 will begin bubbling out through the water. Depending on how much sugar is available, it should continue bubbling for one to two weeks.

Since CO_2 is heavier than air, you must place the end of the hose near the top of the growroom above your plants—that's the reason for its length. When the bubbling stops, dump the alcohol and water out and repeat the process.

You will have only the cost of the sugar and the yeast every week or two. This expense can be cut even further by using this setup only during the flowering stage of growth.

When your plants start out, there will be plenty of CO_2 available. As they get larger and near the flowering stage, they will be using more, so use your judgment as to when to start supplementing them.

DETERMINING PLANT SEX

Once your plants are six weeks old, they are ready to have their sex determined. This is also when you will start keeping them under an MH lamp rather than fluorescents. Some people like to start the plants under the MH as soon as they are placed into the 5 1/4" squares. Waiting until they are about four weeks old will save you a little electricity. As these plants will be your mammas, you will want to start growing them with a more powerful light source at this time. If you are growing a small crop and have only one or two mammas, you will only need a 150w, 175w or 200w MH. If you are growing any more than that, you will need at least a 400w MH, or even a 1000w MH, if you are growing several mammas in a greenhouse setup.

Special Technique

Regardless of the size of the container in which you have germinated your seedlings, we suggest that in order to prepare the seedlings for "sexing" you place them in a larger container. (We use a standard plastic cup sized 5 1/4" wide by 5 1/4" deep. If you move them to a larger container we suggest the use of a B1 transplanting aid and root stimulant. You should not clone a plant directly after transplanting. Wait a few days until the plant has had time to adapt to its new environment.

You should transplant a cutting only from your best parent seedling. Select seedlings which have demonstrated the best overall growth—those with the best foliage, healthy thick stalks and robust root growth. If a parent seedling is small and underdeveloped it probably won't grow into a plant suitable for your needs.

For the special technique for determining plant gender, take a clone of the young parent seedling and place it into a proper environment, then reduce the light period of the clone—but not that of the parent seedling. In three weeks the clone will show gender. As long as you know which parent seedling the clone was taken from, you will then have successfully determined the sex of your plants.

Cloning

Cloning your plants is a simple process. You will need some standard items:

1. **A very sharp blade (a single-edged razor blade or X-acto® knife**
2. **Cloning solution**
3. **B1**
4. **Stickers**
5. **Root cubes, small peat-moss cups or small plastic cups filled with the standard soil mixture**
6. **A plastic tray for storing the root cubes or peat cups**

In order to determine the gender of each plant, we will simply take a cutting, just as you would from an ordinary houseplant—cut off one of the tips and put it in a cup of water. It will soon develop roots and, put in some soil, will become a new plant. Clone from each parent seedling and root the clone into a medium. We will then reduce the light period of the clone only, and in a few weeks it will show gender and thus indicate the gender of its parent seedling.

Again, you take a cutting from a marijuana plant by selecting the top three to four inches of the parent seedling, then with the sharp object cut off the selected tip. Take the tip of the plant between your thumb and index finger and pick another spot about three or four inches down from the tip of the plant. Be sure to select a spot directly above the next node. (A node is the place on the plant's main vertical stem where the lateral branches and food leaves are located. The internode is the space between the nodes.) You will want to make a cut just above the selected node, being careful not to damage the rest of the plant. Make the cut at a 45 degree angle. If it was made properly your clone should have a small bit of stem, about an inch to an inch and a half, at the bottom. The clone is immediately dipped into a cloning liquid, powder or gel, then immediately placed into a water-filled container. The stem must immediately be placed in water or it could develop an air bubble which would kill it. These cloning liquids, powders or gels are helpful in reducing fungal growths on the stems of your new clone.

A clone will develop roots if you simply place it into a glass of water. There are a number of different mediums which may be successfully used to grow your clones. You could use rockwool, root cubes, a standard soil mixture, perlite or a perlite-vermiculite mixture.

If you are using peat cups or plastic cups, make a hole in the soil first before placing the clone into the container. If you shove the tip of the stem through the soil without a prior hole, it will damage the fragile stem of the new clone. You need only place the stem in the soil as deep as the first set of leaves on the clone. That means the first node up from the bottom tip of the clone. The 1" of water in the tray will be sufficient for the clones either in peat-moss cups or plastic containers.

If you use rockwool or root cubes you also place them in water. We have found that small 10 1/2" by 21" wide, 3" deep plastic trays are perfect for this. The trays are filled with water, so that when the clones are put in the trays the tip of the stem will always be in about one inch of water. If you use a mixture, such as 50-50 perlite-vermiculite, you will want to put it into small containers such as peat cups or plastic cups. You will then place the containers into small water-filled trays also. Regardless of the medium you use, make sure that the stem of the clone reaches to the bottom of the container. This will ensure that the developing roots of the clones are always in at least one inch of water. The advantage of placing the containers into the small trays is that it makes changing the water each day easy. You simply pour the old water out and fill the tray with fresh water.

You should add the recommended amount of B1 to your water, place the medium you have selected into the tray, then fill the tray with water, one inch deep. Take your clone, dip it into the rooting solution and immediately place it into the medium which is already in the tray of water. The tip of the stem of the clone will then be submerged in the water.

You do not have to reduce the light period of the parent seedling. Simply keep it under the 18-hour-a-day light period it has been under since the beginning of its germination. As you take a clone from its parent seedling and place it into a tray you will want to indicate which clone came from which seedling. This may be accomplished by placing a sticker on your first clone and marking it #1. Mark its parent seedling as #1 also. Then when the clone shows gender you will know which parent it came from and can thus determine the latter's sex. Continue to do this until all of your parent seedlings have been cloned and labeled (#2, #3, etc.).

Once you have filled up a tray with clones from your parent seedlings, place it in your cloning area under the 40w fluorescent grow tubes and reduce the light to only 12 hours a day. The clones will now remain on the cloning table until they show gender. This will take about 14 days. Their care is quite simple. Using electric timers on the lights, give them 12 hours of light each day. Once every day change the water in the trays. Make sure to keep the room temperature around 75° to 80°F with the exhaust system running. If the clones should show any signs of needing fertilizer around the second week (yellowing of lower food leaves), feel free to give them a 1/4 to 1/2-strength standard fertilizer.

After about 14 days on the cloning table, most of the clones will have grown roots and some foliage, but most importantly, the majority of them will be showing gender. The male and the female plant at first seem to look alike, but once you have learned the determining factors you will be able to identify them easily. Remember, the plants are photoperiodic, and with their light reduced to only 12 hours a day, they will in about two weeks "go to seed" or show gender. It is a simple matter to look at your stickers—the ones which you have marked #1, #2, #3, etc.—and determine which parent seedling your clone came from, since you labeled them identically. You will throw away all your male parent seedlings and male clones and keep all your female parent seedlings.

MALE PLANTS DEVELOP SMALL PODS, WHICH PRODUCE POLLEN. IF YOUR FEMALE PLANTS ARE POLLINATED BY MALE POLLEN, THEY WILL GROW SEEDS. SUPERIOR MARIJUANA IS KNOWN AS SINSEMILLA, OR UNSEEDED POT. BEGINNER GROWERS WILL NOT WANT TO KEEP ANY MALE PLANTS IN THEIR GROW ROOM, SO AS SOON AS A MALE PLANT CAN BE IDENTIFIED, IT SHOULD BE REMOVED AND DESTROYED.

Identifying the Male

The male indicators usually begin to appear towards the top of the plant. If you look closely there or at the axis of the nodes near the top of the plant, you will see the first indicators.

The male plant will start producing a round, slightly pointed oval-shaped or ball-shaped pod. The pod is about 1/4" and is usually yellow, light green or could even have a reddish hue. It starts out as a small bud-like growth but soon forms little stalks as it begins to develop into clumps. The clumps hang downward as more develop. The staminate calyxes soon open to display little banana-shaped pollen sacks or stamens. These pollen sacks can be seen hanging from the center of the male "flower" from small stalks. It is usually fairly easy to identify a male plant before the stamens release any pollen. The clustering effect along with the fact that the male "flower" is at the tip of a small stalk is ample indication of a male plant.

You should destroy all of your males as soon as you identify them. The only exception is if you want to breed for seeds.

If you are interested in collecting pollen for the production of seeds it is very simple to do. First, pick out your very best and healthiest male plant. Once the pollen sacks have started to release pollen, place a plastic bag over the head of the plant and bending the plant downward, give it a gentle but vigorous shake. The pollen may be stored in the freezer for a couple of years if stored with care. Use a good container to prevent freezer burn. Packaging it with a dessicant will help to keep it dry as well.

A FEMALE PLANT WILL DEVELOP TINY WHITE HAIRS. ONCE YOU KNOW A PLANT IS FEMALE, YOU HAVE THE BEGINNING OF A SUCCESSFUL GROW ROOM.

Identifying the Female

At first, the female primordia flower will look very similar to the male. It begins its flowering at the tip of the growing terminals, and develops at the lower nodes of the plant, where the stem and the leaf join. In the beginning, the female flower has a pod-shaped appearance.

One of the main differences you will notice is that the female pod, called a "bract," does not grow out and extend itself on a small stalk or stem as the male does. It stays close to the place it is growing from and forms small and ever-enlarging clusters of "bracts" which in turn develop into "buds." The main difference you will notice is that the females soon develop two 1/4- to 1/2-inch tiny white "hairs" growing directly out of the center of each pod or "bract." These hairs are the sticky pollen-collecting stigmas. They may sometimes be pink or even purple and form a "V" for Victory (which is what we should all strive for as we attempt to have marijuana decriminalized and legalized). The stigma are attached at the ovule inside the base of the calyx.

The female plant is easily identified by its long, white pistils protruding from their pistillate calyx. If your clone is female, keep the parent seedling and discard the clone.

Hermaphrodites

You must always be on the lookout for hermaphrodites. These are plants that for some reason have developed both staminate (male) and pistillate (female) gender. In other words, they display both sexes. These can destroy a crop by pollinating your not-yet mature clones in the area, preventing them from reaching their mature blooming stage. If you find a plant that has both sexes, remove it immediately. These plants will cause you nothing but trouble. Throw it and its parent seedling away.

You must look for these hermaphrodites at every stage of your project but be especially attentive to the plants in the blooming room.

Developing Strong Females

Your plants should now be somewhere around eight weeks old. You have thrown away all your males and have nothing but females left. Your females have never had their light reduced so they will now have grown to the height of about two feet and are called mammas. They are ready to be pinched again to create more growing terminals. Simply pinch 1/4" of the tip of each branch.

You will continue to pinch and grow your female plants until they have about 20 growing terminals each. Once this has been achieved you are ready to start your mass production of clones.

After the cuttings have been taken from the parent seedlings and are placed under the metal halide they will have certain requirements while you are waiting for the sex of the clones to be determined. They will need 18 hours of metal halide light every day. Once under the MH lamp they have a tendency to dry out more quickly than before, which simply means that you will have to water them more often. The plants will probably appear to need more nutrients about a week after the cloning, so give them a standard fertilization. If you can't tell whether they need one or not, give them a 1/4-strength or 1/2-strength fertilization.

The temperature of the grow room should be kept as close to 75 or 80 degrees as possible. The exhaust system should be on. The plants will, for the most part, grow themselves while you are waiting for the gender to be determined.

Mammas

This stage of your project is very simple. You will select the very best of your female plants and discard the rest. This, of course, can only be accomplished if you have extra plants left over at this stage of the growing process. If you don't have as many as you need, take your best females and clone them. These transplants will now grow into mature plants that can be treated as if they grew from seed.

These female plants will become the "mother plants" (or mammas), which means they will "give birth" to the clones, or cuttings, that will be trimmed from them every two weeks.

Around this time you will want to transplant your mammas into larger containers. I place them in 5-7 gallon peat moss or plastic buckets. Fill the larger buckets almost full with the standard soil mixture, water the soil with regular water, place your fingers over the top of the soil (around the base of the stem), turn the 5 1/4" square container upside down and give it a sharp but gentle shake downward. This will remove the plant from the smaller square. Make a depression in the soil of the 5-7-gallon bucket and place the plant into it, making sure not to bury the stem any deeper into the soil than it was in the 5 1/4" square. Water with B1 and you are set.

YOU WLL NOTICE THAT SOME FEMALE SEEDLINGS ARE BETTER THAN OTHERS. YOU SHOULD ONLY KEEP THE BEST FEMALES AS MOTHER PLANTS.

The mammas should be allowed to dry out for a few days between each watering—this means letting the top few inches of the soil dry completely. Once you have watered don't water again until your plant needs it.

The growing terminals are "pinched" once every 10 days or so. These mammas are placed back under their 18-hour-a-day light schedule and grown until they are large enough to give you as many clones as you want. As they grow and are pinched, multiple new growing terminals will develop.

These mammas will be a constant source of supply for clones, replenishing the plants in individual sections of the blooming area every two weeks. As the mother plants grow they will get larger and have many growing terminals. This will help when you want to do some constructive pruning. Determine how many clones you want a certain plant to give on your next cloning. Pick however many you need of the best prospective clones and prune all the other branches. Constant awareness of pruning needs will give you a small, squat mamma that has a flat top instead of a pointed one.

After many months of being a productive mamma, a plant may begin to get root-bound (having too many roots for a given space) or it may develop too long of a trunk. I like to start fresh new mammas about once every six to eight months. You should use the best, healthiest, most productive, bug- and disease-resistant, stoniest mamma for your next generation. You may want to keep the best of a few different types of strains growing. It is a good idea to maintain a small genetic diversity in your crop structure just in case you run into a problem later with your main breed.

Summary

Setting Up

- You chose your seeds carefully, mixed the standard soil solution and started germinating the seeds. When the majority of your seeds were germinated, only the best of them were used.

• You made sure the soil was clean and free of bugs. (You don't want to start off your project with an infestation.) You kept hoods or plastic covers over the trays (containing the 5 1/4" containers), so there is high humidity for the seedlings as they germinate, but not in the entire area or room.

• Whether you used root cubes, soil or another germination medium, you kept the seedlings saturated with water until they germinated. Once you had root development, you slacked off on the watering but kept the soil moist—not dry and not saturated. You made sure the exhaust system was on, and took the hoods or covers off of the germinating seeds once they developed roots.

• You raised the fluorescent lights as the plants grew, and kept them as close as possible to the tops of the plants without burning them.

• After the seedlings developed good roots you transplanted them into 5 1/4" squares, then placed them under metal halide lamps and let them grow 12-14" high, then determined their gender.

• Once your plants were about six weeks old, you gave them their first fertilization and started them on a regular schedule. You also gave them their first application of SuperThrive. Even if your plants didn't look like they needed any fertilizer, you started them on their schedule at the six-week mark.

• You selected the best of your parent seedlings to have their sex determined, and you made sure the plants you took the cuttings from had at least three or four major nodes remaining after the cloning.

• The cuttings were dipped in cloning solution and immediately placed in the growing medium. You made sure that the trays had at least 1" of standing water. You also made sure that you knew which clone came from each parent seedling by tagging them properly with stickers or some other means.

• You placed the parent seedlings back under a metal halide light for 18 hours a day while putting the clones under 40-watt fluorescent grow lights and reduced the light period of the clones to only 12 hours of light per day. You also made sure that electric timers were added to all of the lights. The temperature in the room was kept at around 75 to 80 degrees Fahrenheit.

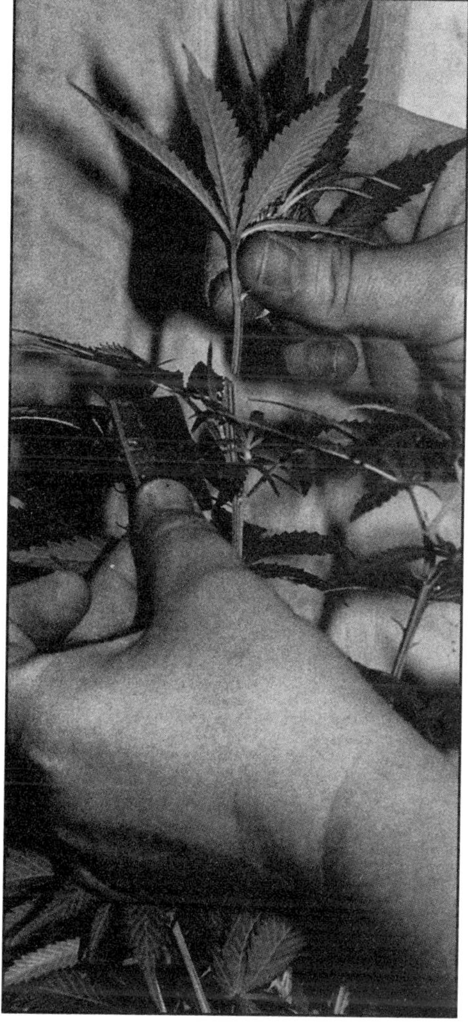

EACH MOTHER PLANT CAN PRODUCE AS MANY AS 30 CLONES EACH MONTH.

Maintenance

• Change the water in the trays every other day, and mist the clones a few times a day. (They appreciate it and, it helps to get moisture into the plantlets. Since they don't have any roots, this is a nice alternative way to receive water.)

• Make sure the clones get only 12 hours of fluorescent light each day.

• Determine the gender of your plants, and keep your eye out for hermaphrodites. Keep pinching the parent seedlings to grow more and more growing tips.

• Your parent seedlings should be around eight weeks old. The remaining females will be mammas. Remember the soil has to breathe when watered. Water and let your soil dry and "breathe" between watering.

• This would be a good time to plant some garlic around the base of your mammas. Check them with a strong magnifying glass for bugs.

CLONING

You will now fill up the first section of your blooming area. For this you will require the same items you needed for cloning your seedlings:

1. **Some trays**
2. **Containers (peat moss cups or plastic containers)**
3. **Medium root cubes or standard soil mixture**
4. **Sharp blade**
5. **B1 transplanting aid**
6. **Anti-fungal rooting powder, liquid or gel**
7. **Hole punch for soil 1/4" wide (such as a chopstick)**

Follow the standard cloning procedure. Make sure you make your cut at a 45-degree angle to the stem, cutting about three inches below the node. Immediately dip the cut lower tip of the clone into the B1 transplanting aid and place it in the medium of your choice. Remember to insert the tip of the stem almost to the bottom of the medium and the 1" of standing water. Also make sure to pre-punch any holes in the soil so you don't damage the fragile stem of the new clone.

For the greenhouse or large setup: If 1/6 of the blooming area will hold 192 plants in 5 1/4" squares (in a 6' X 8' section), then you will want to cut about 200-220 clones every two weeks. This will give you a few extra clones, so you can pick the best 192 and use them. In order to produce 220 clones once every two weeks you would need 10-12 mammas, assuming that each mamma produces 20 cuttings at each cloning.

For the smaller or "closet" setup: You will be attempting to fill 1/4 of your blooming area with clones, which will require 20-30 clones every three weeks. You would need two large mammas producing 10-15 cuttings at each cloning, or one smaller mamma which is capable of generating 20 cuttings every two weeks, to meet these requirements.

I have found that the cloning goes faster if I have all my equipment nearby and all soil mixtures prepared before I start cutting.

When cloning you should always use a sharp, clean instrument. I like to use single-edge razor blades, as I'm less likely to cut myself. An X-acto knife is also useful for this procedure, since the blade is very sharp and the long handle makes it easy to handle.

Cut the best 10-20 growing terminals from your best mamma. If the plant has more than 20 growing terminals prune off any that look weak and throw them away. If your plant doesn't quite have 10-20 growing terminals just cut as many good clones as possible. Cutting will create more potential clones on each plant as time goes on.

Continue to cut terminals, dip them in rooting aid, and then transplant into the soil-filled container (or other growing medium such as vermiculite). Do this until the cloning area is filled up with the transplanted cuttings. Then wait for two weeks as they develop roots and grow. During this time keep them in the standard environment: temp. 75-80 degrees, 18-hours-a-day fluorescent grow lights, air exchange. Change standing water every two days (48 hours), but after six days the standing water is not required. Just keep the cuttings moist for the second week.

An oxygen supplement (Safer's, 1-2-1, Oxygen Plus) will help get more oxygen to the rootless clones. Using a mixture of vermiculite, B1 and an oxygen supplement, I have been able to achieve a 98% survival rate for the clones.

Care and Feeding of the Clones

After you have finished cutting and transplanting and have placed your clones in the cloning area, return the mother plants to their area of the grow room. If you are keeping the mammas under a 150-400-watt metal-halide lamp, make sure that if the light is stationary, the bottom is kept at least two feet away from the plant tops. (A 150-watt MH can be kept as close as one foot from the top of the plants.)

During the two weeks the clones develop roots, you will notice certain things happening to your mammas. They will grow a few inches, if not more, and each growing terminal you previously cut will develop even more potential clones below the cut you made on their nodes. When you cut the tip of a branch it stimulates the lateral growth on the nodes directly below the cut. After the mother has two weeks of regrowth, you'll have twice as many clones. After a while you will have to prune your mammas to keep them the size you require for your available space. Without pruning, the plant will develop many more tops than you need. Too many growing terminals will hinder your efforts. Keep your plants pruned so that they have an average of 20-30 growing terminals at one time.

As the weeks go by I like to fertilize the mammas once every two to three weeks. You will notice that directly after a fertilizing the plants have a growth spurt, and look fresh and green. After a few weeks this diminishes until you notice that the plants don't look as green or seem to be growing as fast. This means it's time to fertilize again. After a while you will be able to tell when your mammas need fertilizer just by knowing their schedule and looking at them.

For preventative maintenance, give the mother plants a light dusting of diatomaceous earth, then two weeks later give them a light spraying with an organic pyrethrum. Diatomaceous earth is made of diatoms, small organic particles that clog the breathing portals and other parts of insects. The diatoms will choke bugs to death. Although it is not a poison, like a chemical pesticide, nonetheless it is not healthy for humans to breathe it. It can be useful for spraying on mother plants and pre-flowers and can be used in the blooming room before flowering sets in. However, do not use this on any budding plant. It is available at most nurseries.

Two weeks after spraying with the pyrethrum, give a light dusting of diatomaceous earth, then two weeks later a spraying with an organic pyrethrum, changing from one pesticide to the other every two weeks. This will insure that your plants stay free of pests, and that no bugs have a chance to obtain a foothold on any of your mammas. This is very important because this is where all future clones will come from. After a clone has been made it is not usually around long enough to get a bug infestation.

Rooting

THIS IS WHAT A CLONE SHOULD LOOK LIKE AFTER TWO WEEKS IN THE CLONING AREA. IT HAS DEVELOPED ROOTS AND IS READY TO BE TRANSPLANTED.

After two weeks under the fluorescent lights most of your clones will have developed roots to some degree.

Whatever growing medium you use, make sure that the lower tip of the clone, which you place into the medium, is placed all the way down into the container, root cube, rockwool, or whatever. This assures you that the tip of the clone will remain immersed in the 1" of standing water that I have recommended for all cloned plants. After one week, standing water is no longer required in the tray, but the entire medium must always remain moist.

If you are rooting in soil and the plants are in cups or containers, it won't be as easy to notice root formation. Sometimes the roots will grow through the peat moss cups or out the drain holes of the plastic containers, but often there will be no way to tell if the clone has developed roots. In general, if a clone has been growing in a container for two weeks and it looks healthy it's safe to transplant it into the larger 5 1/4" container. Also, a gentle tug on the stem of the clone after it has grown in a peat moss cup or plastic container for two weeks will indicate if it has developed a root structure. Resistance to the tug is indicative of root growth.

Maintaining the inch of standing water in the trays is not required after the first week, but make sure the growing medium is moist at all times. If there is excess water in the plant trays after watering it should be poured out.

Transplanting the Clones

After two weeks of tending your clones and mammas it will be time for your second cloning. Thc first thing you will do is clear the cloning area. The first set of clones will need to be transplanted into 5 1/4" squares and moved to the pre-flowering area.

The equipment you will need is:

1. 5 1/4" plastic square containers.
2. Standard soil mixture.
3. B1 transplanting aid.

Transplanting is very simple. Fill a bucket with the standard soil mixture, then scoop some soil into the 5 1/4" container. Fill the container to about 1/2" inch from the top, and water lightly. Then make a depression into the soil of the square large enough to receive the clone.

AFTER CUTTING A CLONE FROM THE MOTHER PLANT, DIP IT IN SOME ROOTING POWDER BEFORE TRANSPLANTING IT INTO A NEW CONTAINER.

Using Root Cubes

Make a small depression in the soil and place the root cube into it, at least one inch under the soil. Then water with the recommended amount of B1. The square with its new plant is then placed under a metal halide in the pre-flowering area where it will receive 18-hour-a-day light.

Using Soil-Filled Containers

Whether your clones are in peat moss cups or plastic containers filled with the standard soil mixture, you will still do the same thing—fill your 5 1/4" square about 3/4 full with soil. You will use less soil because the peat cups and plastic squares take up more space than the root cubes. Lightly water your squares and make a small depression in the soil large enough to receive the clone.

If your roots have not grown through the sides of the cups you may remove the clone from the peat cup and plant it directly into the square. If the roots are anchored into the sides of the peat cups then just place the latter directly into the square, press down firmly but gently, then cover with a thin layer of soil. The top of the peat cup should be about 1/4" below the surface of the soil. Water with B1 and place the square in the pre-flowering area.

The same basic procedure should be followed if your clones are in plastic containers. Place your fingers on the top of the soil at the base of the stem. Invert the container and give it a gentle shake downward. This will usually dislodge the clone from the container. Place the clone into the soil and press firmly but gently around the plant, then add B1 and place the container into the pre-flowering area.

The Second Cloning

Once you have transplanted all the clones the cloning area will be empty. What shall we do about that? Do a second cloning of the mammas to fill the 1/4 to 1/6 of the blooming area, of course. You will notice that since the first cloning two weeks earlier the mammas have grown considerably and sprouted a number of new growing terminals to cut. This is exactly what you will do. Following the standard procedure, you will now take your second set of clones. You now have your cloning area and your pre-flowering area filled.

Continue to establish the standard environment in your work area: keep the air circulating, maintain a 75-degree temperature, continue to water, fertilize the plants, keep the lights on schedule, etc. Familiarize yourself with all the environmental conditions of your area keeping in mind the requirements of your plants. If you are not sure about something simply refer to the first part of the book, General Instructions.

You will continue to repeat the process of cloning once every 14 days, filling up 1/4 to 1/6 of the entire blooming area until the entire area is filled. But let's not get too far ahead of ourselves.

Summary

• Clone the first section of your project. If you have any weak-looking branches or growing terminals, prune them from your mammas. Cut the healthiest growth following the standard cloning procedure.

• Change the standing water in the trays every other day. After about a week or so you will not need to keep an inch of standing water in the trays. After seven days the growing medium only needs to be kept moist.

• As a preventative measure you may want to start the schedule of spraying with organic pyrethrum. Spray in the morning and wash off with a good, fine mist of water the first thing next morning. Two to three weeks later apply a fine dusting of diatomaceous earth. Alternate the applications.

• After the clones develop roots (which takes approximately two weeks), transplant them into 5 1/4" plastic squares (or similar container). Be sure to use B1 transplanting aid and standard soil mixture. Make a hole in the soil of the square and place the rooted clone only up to the top of the growing medium. Do not bury the clone's stem too deep.

• Clone the mammas again. Check all your standard environmental conditions frequently: air flow, temperature, fertilizing, light, bugs, moisture, etc. You will now have mammas, your cloning area filled and your pre-flowering area filled.

• When cloning, make sure that the stem of the clone goes to the bottom of the medium you are placing it into.

• Keep your lights as close as possible to the plants in the pre-flowering area. However, make sure that you reduce the distance to the light gradually. Lower the light a few inches, then wait a few days and see how it affects the plants before you lower it any more.

THE CLONES REQUIRE ONE INCH OF STANDING WATER IN THEIR TRAYS FOR THE FIRST SIX OR SEVEN DAYS. AFTER THE FIRST WEEK, POUR OUT ANY STANDING WATER, BUT CONTINUE TO KEEP THE SOIL MOIST. WATER SATURATION WILL HELP THE CLONES DEVELOP ROOTS.

Cloning and Pre-flowering Tips

1. When cutting clones be sure to use as sharp an object as possible. Use a fresh razor blade or X-acto® knife every time you cut.

2. Make the cut at a 45-degree angle, and cut downward.

3. Keeping one inch of standing water in the trays of freshly-cut clones is important, but it must be kept warm. Cold water inhibits growth. Heating pads that will maintain a warm temperature for plant trays are available at many garden stores. (Do not use other heating pads—they will cause an electrical short and possible electrocution from the water.)

4. An excellent medium to start clones in is 100% small-grain vermiculite. They can be transplanted into the potting-soil mixture after they root.

5. After one week, by which time the clones have developed a strong hydraulic draw of water up the stem, they no longer need standing water. This is a good time to transfer them to clean trays for a second week of developing roots.

6. When transplanting a clone, be sure not to tear or damage the fragile roots, and always use a transplanting aid (such as B1) when moving them into new containers.

7. Preflowers need as much light as possible before being transferred into the blooming area. Some growers use as much as 24 hours of light. I still recommend 18 hours on, 6 hours off. But make sure that all the preflowers are receiving plenty of direct light.

8. As the preflowers grow taller, trim any small, lower branches that look like they won't be good producers.

9. A fan or ventilation system that blows fresh air on preflowers during the lighting hours will create cellulose growth in the stem and make the plant strong.

10. Rearrange your preflowers about every three or four days. Place the faster-growing plants to the edge of your lighting area and the smaller plants directly under the light.

PRE-FLOWERING

Light

Once you have transplanted your first clones into the 5 1/4" squares and placed them in the pre-flowering area, they will have certain requirements. Remember that the area for the mammas and the cloning and pre-flowering areas are all on an 18-hour-a-day light schedule. Like the area set up for mammas, the room set up for flowering should be lit by a metal halide (MH) or high-pressure sodium (HPS) light.

The goal is to get as much growth as possible during the two weeks the plants are in the pre-flowering area. If you are using a stationary 150-400 watt metal halide you will keep the bottom of the light fixture between 12" and 24" above the tops of the plants. If the metal halide is on a motion system you should place it closer—about 6 to 12 inches from the tops of the plants. If you are using a 1000-watt lamp keep the stationary distance about 24-28" from the tops.

A metal halide will give your plants the best growth during this time. The growth spurt they receive from the metal halide will not stop until a week after they have had their light period reduced in the blooming area.

Growth

The area dedicated to preflowers (which is when clones have developed roots but before they have developed buds), is 10' by 4' and will contain approximately 200 clones in the greenhouse-sized area, and 4' by 4' with 20 clones in the small "closet" setup described earlier in the book. Once the clones have been transplanted into the 5 1/4" squares they should not need any fertilizer until they are moved into the blooming area. (When the cuttings are transplanted into the new soil, the fertilizer in the fresh soil should have enough nutrients to last for two weeks.) If you feel the need to add some nutrients (perhaps during the first week after transplanting), use only a 1/4-strength fertilization, then wait a few days to see if that is sufficient before adding any more. But my rule of thumb is that it is usually best not to fertilize a plant for at least one week after it has been transplanted.

After cutting and transplanting the clones, and then placing the plants under 18 hours a day of metal-halide light for two weeks, they should grow to a height of approximately 12" to 18". Then they should be moved into the blooming room or area. They will require the standard care you give all your plants. Make sure the soil in the squares has dried out slightly before watering. To maintain the light schedule accurately, use an electric timer. The growth of your plants while they are on the pre-flowering table will be determined by how well you maintain their environmental conditions. Follow the standard procedures and they will all grow properly.

Sizing

After the plants have been in the pre-flowering area for two weeks and the second set of clones have developed roots, it will be time for the next round of cloning. You will notice that the mammas are slightly larger and have even more growing terminals, and the stems of the terminals will be thicker. In fact, you may notice that some of your mammas have many more growing terminals than you need. We now must consider sizing the mother plant by pruning all the lateral branches that you don't need. First, determine how many growing terminals you require from any particular mamma, then decide which terminals are the best (examine which parts of the plants are producing the healthiest-looking growth) and cut off any branch that is not needed.

This is done for a number of reasons. Extra growth uses energy which should go to the parts of the plant you are using. Extra foliage blocks light which should be directed to the parts of the plant you will be using. Your mamma will now be easier to tend to. The room will also be a healthier environment—after all, the area for the mammas is only so big. Creative pruning will keep them at a more conducive size for the space allocated to them.

Propagation

The self-propagating function of the Sea of Green method will allow you to produce clones once every two or three weeks for an indefinite period of time. You will be able to fill the blooming area as many times as you wish for this reason: every two weeks you will fill up your blooming area with 1/4 to 1/6 more clones. By the time the blooming area is filled, the first clones you made will be almost ready to harvest.

Now you will move the first set of plants you cloned, which are the ones on the pre-flowering table, into the blooming room. You should place only as many plants into the blooming area as is required to fill up 1/4 to 1/6 of the space. If you have more than you need, use only the best and throw away the rest.

You then take the clones from the cloning area and place them into the 5 1/4" squares. Follow the same procedure as the last time you did this. Then clone the mammas again and fill up the cloning area for the third time using the standard cloning procedure. Then repeat, repeat, repeat.

Summary

• The pre-flowering area has a special purpose. You want to grow your plants with as much light and get them as large as possible during the time they are there. This is why they are placed under a metal-halide light. You may want to give the plants a fertilizing about a week after they are transplanted into the 5 1/4" square containers. A 1/4-strength fertilizing followed by another will assure that you will not burn your plants while giving them ample food for growth. Any time your plants show signs of over-fertilization, discontinue until they show signs of needing nutrients again.

• Your plants should grow to a height of about 12" to 18" while they are in the pre-flowering area. Keep the light on an electric timer. Let the squares dry out a bit before watering again.

• After two weeks, clone your mammas again. Remove the rooted clones from the cloning area, transplant them into 5 1/4" squares that are in the pre-flowering area and place them in the blooming area.

• Prune your mammas of any unwanted or weak branches and growing terminals. Make sure that all the proper environmental conditions are applied to each area.

• When you are watering, be very careful that you do not get even one drop on the bulb of your metal halide or high-pressure sodium bulbs.

KEEPING A THERMOMETER IN DIFFERENT PARTS OF THE GROW AREAS WILL HELP YOU TO MAKE SURE THAT THE ENVIRONMENTAL CONDITIONS ARE BEING MAINTAINED PROPERLY. IT'S VERY IMPORTANT THAT PREFLOWERS GROW AS MUCH AS POSSIBLE DURING THE TWO WEEKS AFTER THEY ROOT AND BEFORE THEY ARE PLACED IN THE BLOOMING AREA.

• You have now finished a complete cycle. If you continue to follow this cycle, your project can continue indefinitely. Tend and grow your mammas, tend and root your clones, tend and grow your pre-flowers and continue to do this repeatedly, on schedule, once every two or three weeks. Continue standard maintenance in all aspects of the cloning area.

Max Yields' Cultivation Tips

In addition to helping to edit this book as a consulting editor, Max Yields also dispenses growing advice on the HIGH TIMES Web site (**www.hightimes.com**).

1. Selecting seeds:
It's difficult to judge the viability of a seed by its appearance. There are a few things to look for, however. The seed should not be cracked or broken, and although size doesn't necessarily mean anything, larger seeds got that way by storing more water for the time they will use it to begin a new growth cycle. Because of this, larger seeds may have a better chance when they start, especially under adverse conditions.

2. Making the best use of indoor light:
Making the floor reflective, along with the walls and ceiling, will help to distribute a bit more light to your plants. Keeping the lights as close to the plants as possible (at least one foot away for HID lamps, and one to two inches away for fluorescents), and rotating them periodically will also help. If you have a large grow area, putting your lights on light movers is a good idea as well. Also, change your bulbs regularly. Bulbs lose efficiency and light output as they get older. I recommend changing the bulbs in an HID fixture at least once a year, and those in a fluorescent every six months.

3. Avoiding infrared detection:
When law enforcement uses heat sensing equipment to search for indoor gardens, they are looking for hot spots on the roof or walls of a home—areas where there is an abnormal amount of heat localized in one place. All structures radiate some heat from the walls and roof. What they are looking for, as I said, is hot spots. If you were to drop a ceiling below the actual roof and kept the light beneath it, the space above the ceiling would disperse the heat evenly before it got to the roof. This would eliminate the tell tale hot spot. Good ventilation will also help to disperse some of the heat.

4. Odor control:
Here's an old trick I picked up years ago. Run a hose from the vent fan into a bucket of water mixed with a pine-scented cleanser. When the air bubbles through, it will smell as clean as a freshly mopped floor.

5. Here are a few pieces of advice for any first-time grower.

A. Keep it simple.
Don't try anything too elaborate your first time around. A simple setup will be easier to maintain and manage. Make sure you have enough light, ventilation, circulation, etc., but keep it simple.

B. Don't overdo it.
This kind of follows from "keep it simple." What I mean here is don't make the mistake of thinking that if so much fertilizer is called for, more would be better. Don't overfertilize or overwater to get your plants to grow better. They won't.

C. Be vigilant.
Keep as close an eye on things as possible. Get to know your plants and their habits well. If you do, you'll spot trouble almost before it gets there and have a much better chance of correcting or avoiding it.

D. Be patient.
There is sometimes the temptation to rush things when it's your first time around. Don't. Have a schedule and try to stick to it. If all goes well, it will be worth the wait. And, last but not least...

E. Love what you're doing, every part of it.
Need I say more?

BLOOMING

Light

When your first plants are placed into the blooming area they will begin to change. At first, they will be about 12" to 16" in height, and in a very vegetative mode due to the strong metal halide they were receiving in the pre-flowering area. This means that they will continue to grow for about a week and put on a few more inches before the vertical growth slows.

The light period of the blooming room will be 12 hours of light per day. As soon as the plants start receiving the reduced light they will begin the flowering state—growing buds, which is exactly what you want them to do. To encourage flowering use 400-watt high-pressure sodium bulbs with the proper ballast. These lamps should have glass shields which will prevent water from being splashed on the bulb. Keep the bottom of the light 12 inches from the tops of the plants when it is on an 6' long moving rail. It may be raised or lowered using the chains it is suspended from. If it is stationary I would have it 24" away. If you use a 1000-watt light keep it 24" away from the top of the plant if the light is moving and about 36" away if it is stationary. If any of these distances burn your plants increase the distance immediately. The lights should be kept on schedule by the use of electric timers. (All suggested distances from grow lights are a maximum, and can be adjusted with experience.)

During the dark period in the blooming area make sure that no stray light shines on the plants—this will interrupt their flowering cycle, and encourage them to grow leaves and branches instead of buds. If you must use light in this sensitive area during the 12-hour darkness cycle, use a weak blue light or a weak light with a blue filter. Try to keep the light from directly hitting your plants and keep the exposure time to a minimum.

Spacing

Once your first set of plants is placed in the blooming area it will be two weeks before another set follows. During these two weeks your plants will need some standard maintenance.

I have recommended the use of 5 1/4" square containers rather than round pots because square containers utilize space more efficiently. Fill only one section of your grow room at any given time. This will help to space the timing of each two-week supply of new clones with the timing of your first harvest, as well as every cloning after that.

I try to keep my watering on a regular schedule. Depending on the environmental conditions, a watering should be necessary only once every few days, but you should check your plants as often asyou can—every day if possible. If a few seem extra dry give them a little water to tide them over. Whenever you add fertilizer be sure it coincides with a standard watering. Water your plants with 1/2 the standard amount of water, then put the fertilizer in the remaining water and complete the watering. Using this method will help to reduce the chance of over-fertilizing or burning your plants.

It stands to reason that as each plant grows vertically it will grow wider as well. If a plant grows to the height of 18" to 24" and you feel it is crowding the surrounding plants, trim the lower branches. Do not trim the upper or middle food leaves of the plant in an attempt to get more light to your plant. The flowering plants need the food leaves to produce buds. It's OK if a plant grows wide enough that it touches the edge of another plant. It is acceptable even if the plants' branch tips overlap, but any more growth than that should be trimmed.

The exhaust system must be active to insure a fresh supply of air to your plants. Standard fertilization of the plants should continue with one important change—once your plants have been placed into the blooming room for approximately 14 to 21 days, you should switch from a high-nitrogen fertilizer, which is for the vegetative stage, to a low-nitrogen, high-phosphorus and high-potassium fertilizer, which is more suited to the flowering stage. You will notice that after two to three weeks, the plants will start to show signs of flowering. From this point on give them only the blooming fertilizer. By the fourth week in the blooming area the plants are concentrating most of their energy on forming buds rather than vertical growth and should be anywhere from 16" to 20" in height.

Timing

The entire Sea of Green process depends on a timed schedule. The flowering part of the process must be kept precise. Your schedule may differ slightly from a 14-day schedule. You may be on a 13-day schedule or maybe a 15-day timetable. Keep on whatever daily program you have determined is best for you. For the purposes of describing the Sea of Green process for this book, I have used a 14-day schedule.

Therefore, each and every 14 days certain standard things will happen:

1. Clone your mammas and place the transplanted cuttings in the cloning area.
2. Move the previous two weeks' worth of clones out of the cloning area and into the pre-flowering area, and move the plants that were previously in the pre-flowering area the blooming area.

If your variety takes 12 weeks to bloom, you will fill up 1/6 of your blooming area every two weeks. If your variety takes eight weeks to bloom, you will take clones every two weeks, and fill up 1/4 of your blooming area every two weeks.

From this point on, the project is self-perpetuating. With proper care and the following of all standard procedures you will now harvest 1/4 of the blooming area as long and as many times as you wish.

Summary

• The first plants have been removed from the pre-flowering area and placed into the blooming area, where they will receive 12 hours a day of high-pressure sodium light. Try to position the lights as close to the top of the plants as you can without burning the plants or causing them to "run."

• The plants now begin to flower, because they are reacting to the reduced light period. Do not let any light leak into the blooming area while it is dark.

WHEN THE PLANTS ARE READY FOR THE BLOOMING AREA, ADD A FULL SPECTRUM BLOOMING FERTILIZER (6-30-30) TO THEIR WATER. THIS WILL FEED ALL STAGES OF BLOOMING GROWTH.

• Do not use round containers for this room. Use square containers for maximum efficiency. Every two weeks you will fill 1/4 to 1/6 of the blooming area with healthy clones. Continue to do this until the entire blooming area is filled.

• When you trim the plants, cut only the lower branches from the clones and only those that look like they will not produce well. Do not trim the leaves on the upper part of the clones. Trim leaves from the lower part if they are turning yellow. All other leaves are needed for flowering growth.

• Continue to monitor the environmental conditions. Keep on schedule for all things such as watering and fertilizing. Test your pH frequently. Make sure that your exhaust system works in the entire area, including the cloning area.

• All standard functions of the cloning area for the mammas, the clones and the pre-flowers must be kept in sync with the blooming room.

• Keeping a written diary will help you remember all the things you need to do throughout each cycle. Once the entire blooming area is filled, one more cloning will be taken. The first clones will then be harvested and the new clones put in the place vacated by their harvest. From this point on you will harvest 1/4 to 1/6 of your blooming area as you cut fresh clones from your mother plants.

• Make a list of all the chores you need to do every week or every month and follow them. Look for things that are unique to your particular situation—some things that are not mentioned in this book, such as security concerns unique to your grow room, or use your own intuition and solve all problems unique to your project.

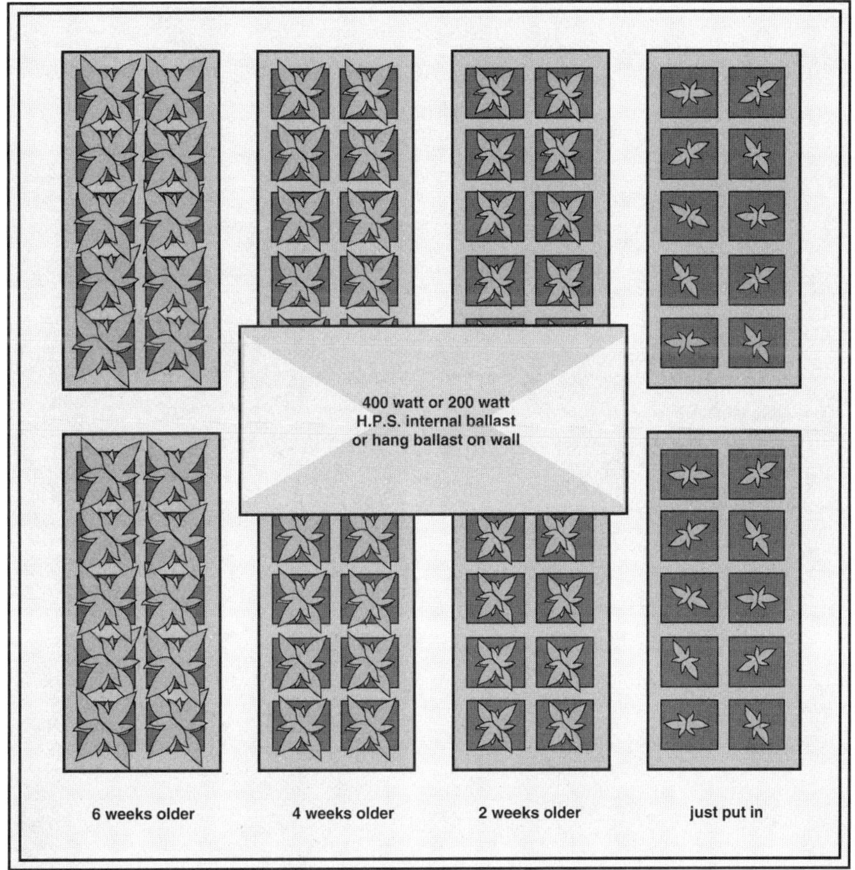

THE BLOOMING ROOM

STANDARD MAINTENANCE

Growing Tips

I think it is best if you can tend to your project first thing in the morning. I usually arrange for the lights to come on at 8 AM in both the cloning area and in the blooming area. (This is done with the aid of electric timers.)

I check the environmental conditions first—the temperature has to be kept around 75 to 80 degrees. You should not let the room temperature drop more than 12 to 15 degrees at night and never below 60 degrees at all. This could mean adjusting an air conditioner or checking a heating unit. I usually readjust the temperature at 8 PM which is the last time I visit the project each day. Sometimes by the next morning the room requirements have changed.

Next, I check the moisture content of the mammas, the clones, the pre-flowers, and then the flowering plants in the blooming area. I keep a written account of all watering and fertilizing schedules of the various areas, which helps me to remember when to do what.

Then I check to see if any bugs or rodents have come into contact with the system. It is a good idea to check your lights with a light meter at least once a week. If you have moving rails, check them to make sure they're functioning properly. Make sure that all electrical systems such as exhaust fans and timers are in good working order.

The proper use of your heating or cooling device, combined with your exhaust fans, will assist in obtaining the proper humidity level. You will want to keep humidity around 50 to 70 percent.

It is a very good idea to take a reading of your pH once every 14 days in the blooming area (See Chapter 3, General Information). If the pH is low, or acidic, simply add two heaping tablespoons of fine dolomite lime and one heaping tablespoon of horticultural hydrated lime to a gallon of water and give a cup or so to each plant. Then check the pH a week later. Slow adjustments are best.

I check the overall quality of the entire process each morning. Then I check all the plants to be sure no bugs have found their way into the area. Keep your eye (and nose) open for molds and fungus.

Wiping down any exposed area, sweeping and mopping will go a long way in keeping a healthy atmosphere for your project. It is a good idea to be clean when visiting the grow room.

As a preventive measure I like to give the plants an application of diatomaceous earth when they are first placed in the blooming room. This is a simple dusting of the plant, done at that time only. I make sure that the undersides of the leaves and crevices of the nodes are dusted thoroughly. Then two weeks later I give the plants a spraying with the organic soap wash Pyrethrum Sabidillia. Make sure that the spray is used on all the undersides of the leaves as well as the tops. Be sure that the crevices of the nodes are sprayed well also—this is a favorite spot for bugs to hide.

I do not give the plants another dusting of the diatomaceous earth two weeks later. The plants in the blooming area only get the treatment once when they are first placed there. Diatomaceous earth will stick to the young developing pistils. Whenever you use it be sure to wear the proper breathing device, and have a fan blowing across your working area and in the direction of an exhaust vent.

Keep your eye out for any hermaphrodites (male plant with female characteristics or a female that also shows male characteristics). They can develop quickly, so you should check for them every day. One hermaphrodite can stunt all of your females. Millions of pollen grains can be released at one time. If a newly flowering plant is fertilized it will stop its flowering and concentrate on developing seeds instead of buds. You should eradicate the entire plant if you find it's a hermaphrodite.

I like to rearrange the flowering plants in the blooming area once every two weeks or so. Moving the taller plants to the edge of the lighted area and the smaller plants to the center will give a more proper distribution of light to each plant. If a plant is too small, you can make it "taller" by putting a suitable object under it.

When watering a plant that is in the flowering stage, it is a good idea not to pour any water on the plant itself. Doing this can damage the fragile resin-producing glands. On the other hand, a light misting once a week with a fine spray will help to keep your plants clean and fresh, as long as there are no fungus or bug problems.

When watering, I pour the water onto the top of the soil in a circle around the base of the stem. (By "on the soil" I mean the outer edge of the container away from the stem itself.) A small depression in the soil around the inner edge of your container will help insure that the stem doesn't get too wet. You should never have a depression around the stem of your plant that could collect water as this will facilitate root rot.

Top Ten Basic Guidelines

Here are a few tips that I have found very useful:

1. You do not have to germinate your seeds in the light. Seeds prefer darkness when germinating. Once they have germinated you should not water the seedlings unless they require it. You should let your medium, which houses the seedlings, dry out on the surface. As long as the bottom of the medium is moist the seedlings should have enough water.

2. When the seedlings have been transplanted into 5 1/4" squares, it is a good time to start them under the metal halide light—usually when they are about four weeks old.

3. When the first seedlings are cloned be sure to place the freshly cut stem all the way into the containers almost to the bottom of the medium. I stop about 1/4" from the bottom.

4. Be sure that the trays always contain at least 1" of standing water the first week after the clones have been placed into them. Change this water every day or two. During the second week (seven days after the clones are placed into the trays), the standing water is not necessary. The grow medium should just be kept moist. Any standing water after the seventh day should be poured out after each watering.

5. Never over-fertilize. It is always better to under-fertilize and then notice a nutrient need than it is to correct a problem from over-fertilization. If you over-fertilize you will damage your soil and plants. If you are not sure if your plants need it or not, don't fertilize them.

6. You must make two separate areas. One area will have an 18-hour-a-day light period, and the other will have a 12-hour-a-day light period. Even if you're growing in a closet, it must have two separate areas.

ALL OF THE SOIL ADDITIVES YOU NEED TO GROW GOOD MARIJUANA ARE SOLD OVER THE COUNTER AT NURSERIES, GARDEN SHOPS, AND LARGE DEPARTMENT STORES EVERYWHERE. JUST REMEMBER: NEVER TELL ANYONE THAT YOU ARE GROWING MARIJUANA WHEN YOU PURCHASE LIGHTS, FERTILIZER, OR OTHER PRODUCTS. DON'T ASK ANY SALESPEOPLE FOR "TIPS" ON GROWING MARIJUANA. MANY GARDEN STORES ARE UNDER SCRUTINY FROM THE DEA AND THE POLICE.

7. If you have a very small project such as a closet system or an attic you still must set up an air exhaust system.

8. Even if you are strongly against using pesticides at any time, the preventive maintenance I suggested for bugs (an initial dusting with diatomaceous earth and a pyrethrum spraying 3-4 weeks later) is your best measure to avoid an infestation. If bugs attack your mammas, you will be forced to use extreme measures to completely eradicate them. In fact, if you can't get rid of the bugs you will have to consider starting your project all over again. This will depend on how damaging the bugs are and if they can be controlled, but an infestation can undo all the hard work, time and money you put into the project.

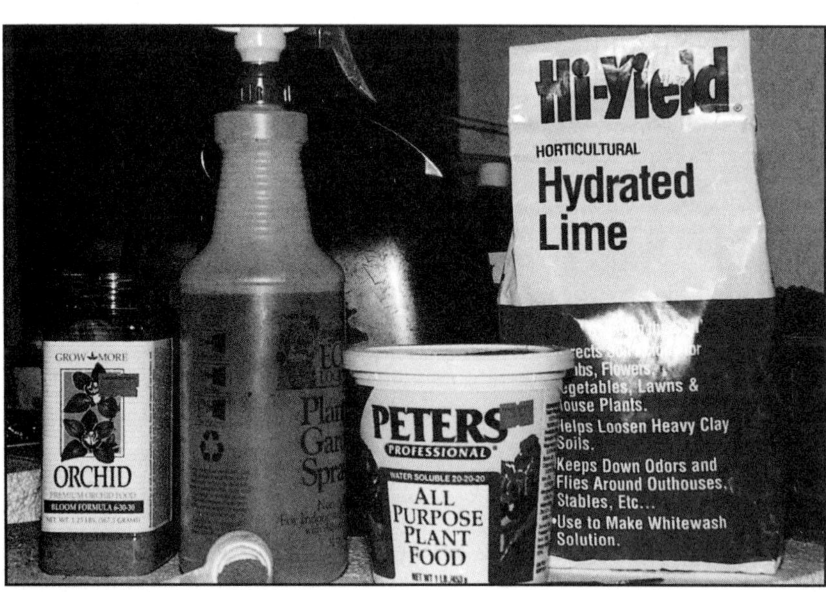

9. If you are on a budget and must reuse either your trays or your 5 1/4" squares, be sure that they are washed with an insecticide soap and a capful of chlorine bleach per gallon of water during the rinse. If you can afford to obtain new containers for each new planting, do so. Allow your mammas, pre-flowers and flowering plants to dry a bit between each watering to allow them to "breathe."

10. Do not fertilize your plants during the last three weeks they are in the blooming area. This could "stress" them. Also, there will be a residual taste of the unused chemicals in the plants that is not healthy to smoke. Finally, I suggest that you let the plants go without water during the last few days before harvest.

Grow Room Checklist

1. Air ventilation
2. Air circulation
3. Humidity (40-50%)
4. Temperature:
   day: 70-75 degrees F
   night: 50-60 degrees F
   (unless the light cycle is set for nighttime)
5. Soil Moisture: water as necessary
6. Cultivate soil surface
7. Check pH
8. Rotate plants
9. Check for spider mites (underside of leaves)
10. Check for fungi or algae
11. Check for nutrient deficiencies
12. Maintain fertilization schedule
13. Check light system for excessive heat at plug and at bulb
14. Check walls and ceiling for mold.
15. Move lamps (2”-12” above the plants)
    fluorescent lights: 2” above the plants
    HID lights: 12” above the plants
16. Clean up all areas before leaving

HARVEST

In nature, during the fall (or harvest) season, the photoperiod is shortened because the amount of sunlight is reduced as the Earth begins to tilt away from the sun. In your grow room it will be the beginning of spring every two weeks as you generate new clones, and the end of fall every two weeks as you harvest.

In your grow room, there will be no timing with cycles of the moon for the harvest. The timing of the entire process is on a two-week schedule, determined by the time it takes your clones to root. My experience with this process and the rooting is that not all projects are the same. Even if two people are trying to do the same, using the same instructions, for some strange reason things come out differently. These variations are like the differences between individual people.

Adjusting the Blooming Area

The plants in your particular system might take three weeks to root. This is not a problem, but you will have to make adjustments in the entire process. That is, if it takes your indoor system three weeks before 90-100% of your clones have developed roots, you simply have to change all the other two-week cycles and plan to do everything in three-week intervals. This will mean that you should clone once every three weeks. The step after rooting (pre-flowering) will also last three weeks instead of two, and finally the harvest will also take place once every three weeks.

The reason is that we have found the average time for plants go into flowering is 8-12 weeks. For the large, greenhouse-sized project the standard time for rooting was two weeks. We divided 2 weeks into the 12 weeks it would take for plants to totally go to flower and came up with 6. Therefore we filled up 1/6 of the blooming area 6 times (once every two weeks). This way, once the blooming area is totally filled (eight weeks), the first clones placed in it will be ready to harvest. This will create space for the next set of clones, which will take the place of the buds that are being harvested.

Let's take a look at a crop that takes three weeks for clones to develop roots, yet takes only eight weeks to completely flower. You will simply fill 1/3 of your blooming area once every three weeks. Divide 3 weeks into the 8 weeks it takes for flowering and you will end up with 2.66. Since this is less than three, you will discover that if the blooming room is divided into three separate parts, this will allow 1/3 of the total area to be filled up every three weeks.

Refer to the diagrams in Section One, Chapter One. The first section will be filled up with the first set of clones. Three weeks later the second section will be filled, and by the sixth week the third section will be filled. By the eighth week, the first section will be ready for harvest. You can wait a week before harvesting, because the clones (on a three-week schedule) and the pre-flowers (also on a three-week schedule) won't be ready to fill the area until the ninth week. If your first bloomers are ready after eight weeks, you will have one week when 1/3 of the blooming area is bare, but you will still be harvesting every three weeks.

If your clone and rooting takes three weeks and your strain takes 12 weeks to harvest, divide 3 into 12 and you'll get 4. This would mean you will fill 1/4 of your blooming area once every three weeks, and your harvest will be every three weeks instead of every two weeks.

Whether yours is a greenhouse or a small closet setup, the comparative size of the cloning and blooming areas will depend on the amount of time that it takes you to root your clones, and the time it takes for the clones to fully bloom. The blooming area will be 4 to 6 times larger than the cloning area since it will be filled with preflowers that will take 8-12 weeks to fully-form the flowers (buds), that you're attempting to cultivate.

That was simple enough, wasn't it? Let me give you one more variable in the formula. It doesn't always take 12 weeks from the time you place your plants into the blooming area until they are ready for harvest. If most of them are ready at this time then you are right on schedule, but if a few plants should be picked a little early, so be it. Like I said: individual differences. If, however you are growing a strain that goes to bloom in about eight weeks, then you will need to make one more adjustment in your formula.

Let's start with the standard process, following the projected time schedules. Say you are cloning and developing roots on a two-week schedule. However you discover it only takes your fast-blooming strain eight weeks to totally develop into buds. No problem. Simply divide your root development time, 2 weeks, into your blooming time, 8 weeks. You will get 4. Therefore once every two weeks you will want to clone enough to fill up 1/4 of your blooming room.

The timing of your harvest starts when you determine how many days it takes to develop roots after cloning from the parent. Most roots will have developed within 14 days of cloning. Sometimes it takes a few days longer. As long as you clone on your own schedule of rooting and fill up 1/6 of your blooming area each time, you will harvest on schedule. If it takes longer to root your clones that simply means that your blooming time will be divided differently. If you should find that your plants in the blooming area are fully flowered by the time that you have filled up only 5/6 (five of the six areas), then divide your blooming room into five separate sections and clone enough each time to fill one section.

Once you have determined how long it takes for your plants to bloom, you may formulate exactly how much of your blooming area needs to be filled, and how often. For a rule of thumb, since your plants will be blooming between 8-12 weeks, use the average time of 10 weeks. If the clones are taking two weeks to root, start by filling up 1/5 of your blooming room at a time, then adjust how much of the space should be filled up or left empty after your first plants bloom. If the clones require three weeks to bloom, you will want to fill 1/3 to 1/4 of your blooming area for the first time. Make adjustments from there.

Signs a Plant is Ready

There is no specific time that we can tell you it is best to harvest, unless someone has told you how long the strain you are growing takes, or you have grown it before. Different strains have different harvest times. On the average it will take 8 to 12 weeks from the time you place your plants into the blooming room until you harvest them.

There are certain indications which will tell you when your plants are ready to harvest. If you are blooming on a 12-week schedule, around the 10th week your plants should be bulbous, with most of their calyxes developed. During the next two weeks, the small pollen-receiving pistils will begin to turn a brownish red. A few small clusters (along the sides of the buds, and especially on the tip) of calyxes will sprout in a final effort to achieve pollination. This will give your buds a refreshed and stretched look. If your buds have pistils that are close to 50% brown, it is time to pick your plant. Some plants in the group will become completely ripe a few days before, or after, the rest. You may notice that 50% of the pistils have turned brown, yet the resin glands are still translucent, and not yet opaque. It is still time to pick.

THIS SINSEMILLA PLANT HAS ALMOST ALL WHITE PISTILS, AND IS ABOUT TWO WEEKS FROM HARVEST. ITS RESIN GLANDS SPARKLE. SOME LOWER FOOD LEAVES ARE TURNING YELLOW, JUST LIKE TREE LEAVES DO IN AUTUMN.

However you determine the blooming time, you have to know the proper signs that indicate that a plant or clone is ready for harvest. You will notice that once you drop the light period and the plants begin to bloom it won't be long before you have a number of nice, full-grown 14" to 18" buds. You will determine that they are full-grown because as you watched their growth you noticed certain things happening. You noticed that the bud got bigger when more calyxes, one on top of the other, were produced, creating bud formations. When these calyxes start to peak out and production slows down, it is an indication that the plant is almost ready to be harvested.

As the calyxes' production begins to slow down, you will notice other things going on: more resin glands (capitate-stalked trichomes) start to appear on the calyxes. These will secrete a small, round, translucent cap of resin on the top of the stalked gland. As the bud ripens some of the resin globs change color from translucent to opaque. You will also notice that, as the production of the calyxes slows down, so does production of the resin glands, and the number of resin caps (round balls) which are opaque will increase. After a while, these round caps will appear on all of the glands, and they're as big as they are going to get. Once most of the calyxes and the resin glands have been produced and the latter are bulbous, the plant is ready to harvest.

Sometimes you'll find that your plants are showing all the signs that they're ready for harvest in the 10th week, two weeks early. Or you'll notice that all the stigmas have turned red yet the heads of the resin glands are still translucent. You may pick at this time, or you may want to let them go a little longer before determining if they are ready. This is up to you. On the other hand, if you notice that all the resin glands have developed as big a cap of resin as they will, and that all the caps have turned opaque, yet not quite half of the plant's stigmas have turned red, I suggest that you harvest at that time. The key indicator is the appearance of the resin glands, and the change from clear to a milky or red color.

You will keep a very close eye on every plant in the blooming room. You will especially want to watch your blooming plants the closer it gets to harvest time. It is not uncommon for blooming plants to form male parts at this time. If you notice this happening either cut off the male parts or remove the entire plant from the area by harvesting it. Be careful not to spread any pollen around if it is in an advanced, pollen-releasing stage.

Experience will teach you just when the right moment has arrived. If this is your first time growing marijuana, you might try experimenting and testing the results to define for yourself when you want to harvest.

MORE OF THE LARGE FOOD LEAVES ARE TURNING YELLOW AS THE PLANT DIRECTS ITS ENERGY TO PRODUCE THE BUDS. HALF THE PISTILS HAVE TURNED RED. THIS PLANT WILL BE READY FOR HARVEST IN A FEW DAYS.

Cutting Down the Plants

Harvesting is easy enough, and a lot of people think this is the "fun" part. Once a plant is ready, simply take some pruning shears, or a sharp blade, and cut each individual plant. Harvest all of your plant. Cut at the base of the stem next to the soil—I cut as close to the soil as possible, as this gives me a "handle." An added advantage is that when I empty the soil containers into the outside garden, I don't have any large stems to contend with.

After cutting I place the buds into a laundry basket and bring them into the drying area. I have found that garbage bags or ziplock bags will crush the buds.

If you are growing off-premises, you might want to transport the buds from the growing site to wherever you want to store them during this process. In that case, put the plants into a suitable container after cutting, then bring them to the drying area.

As I mentioned, I use an outdoor garden to dispose of the soil and leftover plant material. I make a large pile of soil by breaking up the contents of the used containers, and then reuse the soil in the garden. To dispose of the leftover leaves and stems I put them in a fireplace or barbecue pit. I also have a compost pile in the backyard. If you are growing in an urban area, you should plan ahead how to dispose of the soil and plant material. I advise against putting this material into your own garbage cans, since this will tip off your building super and the sanitation crew as to what is going on upstairs.

Drying

The drying process is quite simple. The area for drying should be dark, and will require ventilation. It is absolutely imperative that the drying area have low humidity—a damp area could cause fungus to grow on your drying plants, which will ruin the whole crop. (Buds with fungus should never be consumed or smoked.) If you have a problem with fungus or dampness in your drying area you may want to consider a dehumidifier. The drying area should have a temperature around 90 to 100 degrees. I use a spare room. A closet, basement, or attic (be careful of the heat and humidity in the warmer months) will do.

Drying the plants will add moisture to the air in whatever room or area you place them in, which also encourages fungus. Therefore you will vent the area to remove the excess moisture. I usually open the door or a window a few inches and use a fan to blow air out of the opening.

Here's a little drying tip: If you place the buds inside a plain brown shopping bag while it is laying flat, putting single layers of buds close to the end of the bag, you create a simple drying area. Keeping the brown bags in a drawer or on the shelves in a closet, somewhere dark, can help the drying process. Check the buds and turn them over every day.

With a large harvest, I tie strings from one end of the drying room to the other about six feet above the floor. The plants are hung upside down by draping one of the lower branches over the string. I try to place each plant along the string so that it touches but does not crowd the plant next to it—approximately two inches apart. This allows each plant to have enough space to dry. I keep the rows of drying plants about 10-12 inches apart to create a space for air flow.

BUDS SHOULD BE WELL-MANICURED AND HUNG UP TO DRY IN A WARM, DARK, WELL-VENTILATED AREA FOR A WEEK TO 10 DAYS. THE DRIER, THE HIGHER.

It takes anywhere from five to eight days to completely dry the flowers using this method. I have found the best way to figure out if your buds are dry enough is to smoke one and see for yourself. Before you do that you can usually tell if a group of buds are dry by simply feeling them with your fingers. The outer food leaves should crumble under the pressure of a pinch from your fingers. The buds should feel moist to the touch yet crumble under a strong twisting pinch.

The standard time for drying should be anywhere from a few days to a week or so. You do not want your buds to dry out too fast. (It has been recommended that properly dried buds should retain about 30% of their original weight.) The consistency of the bud should be such that it feels firm and spongy yet when you twist it with your fingers it breaks up into smaller parts rather than just smashes. Notice how it burns in a cigarette, which should stay lit and form a long ash. If you light the cigarette and it goes out within a few seconds and forms a hard ash on the tip then it is not dry enough.

You may find that in some drying areas some parts of the room dry the flowers faster than others. In a room you may find that the closer a plant is to the door the sooner it will dry out. The flowers next to the rear wall may take a little longer to dry. Each plant should be considered dry individually. Don't assume because a couple of plants are dry that all the plants are. I try to find the buds in the drying area that are ready each day and remove them.

Trimming and Manicuring

There are two schools of thought here. Some people prefer to manicure each bud before drying. Keeping the humidity just a bit higher dries the plants slowly and evenly without the risk of too much handling after they are dry. While I prefer to trim and manicure after they dry completely, I do most of the work beforehand. First I trim the plants of all large and unusable leaves soon after harvest. Allowing the buds to dry with large leaves still attached will risk knocking off the dried resin glands and trichomes (which contain the highest levels of THC), if you manicure plants afterwards.

However, by leaving some of the food leaves on the plant during the drying process to shroud the buds they will dry a little bit slower, and a little better. When you remove the outer food leaves before the buds are dry, the outer edge of the bud will dry out more than it should. If you leave the leaf on the bud as it dries out, the outer edge and the inner part of the bud will dry more evenly.

Once the buds have been properly dried the food leaves should be removed. Do not trim your buds to the nub. Removing the larger food leaves may be done by hand or scissors. Take special care not to damage the fragile glands on the buds as you work with them. (This is the reason that some growers manicure before drying.)

Storage

You should store your plants in either glass containers or plastic bags in the vegetable part of your refrigerator or in a place with a similar temperature—around 50 degrees or below, but well above freezing. The buds should be kept out of the light, not handled. If you can seal them in a plastic container such as Tupperware (after extracting as much air out of the container as possible) this will help preserve potency.

Treat the buds carefully—do not smash or crumble them together. Pack them tightly, rolled in plastic if you must—just don't crush them in the packaging.

Smoking

I hope that at the end of your first drying experience you will take your first bud and smoke it. When you do, think about how nice it would be if the rest of the people in the world understood the truth about marijuana. I don't mean that everyone should experience marijuana. I just mean that people should know the truth about it.

I personally hope this book has been helpful to you in some way. It was written for you. I want to wish you the very best of luck on your project. So until we meet again, this is "Hans" saying "adios amigos."

The Sea of Green Series

The Most Popular Growing Guides *Ever*!

THE ORIGINAL!

Sea of Green

The Ultimate "How-to" Cultivation Videotape

Turn your closet into a million dollar growroom! Thousands of people have purchased this tape to learn the easiest instructions on how the Sea of Green process, the easiest and fastest growing technique ever! This 2 hour video now available in :
NTSC (US) CODE: **017V**
PAL (Europe) formats! CODE: **021V**
Originally ~~$79.95~~,
Now Only $29.95!

NEW!

Sea of Green:The Perpetual Harvest **The Perfect Beginner Book!**
Based on the best-selling *Sea of Green* and the new *Sea of Green: The Closet System* videotapes, this book is the perfect companion to either video. It contains lots of tips and detailed information that don't appear in the videotapes.
Only $24.95! H108

NEW!

Sea of Green: The Closet System

Grow Pot in your spare time!

This easy-to-follow video shows how you can harvest 18 to 20 inch buds every two weeks in a space as small as a clothes closet. This tape is especially geared for the home grower who just wants to learn how to grow their stash in a small space like a closet or attic.
Only $29.95

NTSC (US) CODE: **022V**
PAL (Europe) formats! CODE: **023V**

THE SEA OF GREEN COLLECTION

PLEASE SEND ME THE ITEMS I HAVE INDICATED BELOW:

NAME

ADDRESS

CITY STATE ZIP

ITEM#	TITLE	QTY	PRICE	COST

❑ Payment Enclosed* ❑ VISA ❑ MasterCard — SUBTOTAL

*Make check or money order payable to: TRANS HIGH — Add $3.00 shipping $3.00

Card#________ TOTAL

Expiration Date________

Signature________

MAIL COUPON WITH PAYMENT ORDER TO:
TRANS HIGH PRODUCTS
PO BOX 621
Mt. Morris, IL 61054

Please allow 6-8 weeks for processing and delivery.

NMNP/NMP/TB96

GROWERS UNITE!

HIGH TIMES BOOKSTORE

CALL TOLL-FREE FOR ORDERS ONLY
1 (800) 851-7039

Indoor Marijuana Horticulture
Jorge Cervantes' complete and authoritative guide to cultivation.
320 pgs., large format, illustrations and photos.
HB42 $21.95

The Emperor Wears No Clothes
Updated edition of Jack Herer's classic treatise on hemp, its history, and how it can solve many of the world's problems.
246 pgs., large format, illustrations and photos.
HB55 $19.95

How To Build A Bigger, Better Hydro Garden for Under $20
Covers both indoor and outdoor from the perspective of cheap and easy.
94 pgs., illustrated.
HB27 $9.95

The Great Book of Hemp
The latest complete guide to the environmental, commercial, and medicinal uses of hemp.
256 pgs., photos and illustrations.
HB09 $19.95

Marijuana Law
"This book contains the most important things about marijuana law that a user must know," Tony Serra. Indispensable legal reference.
176 pgs.
HB86 $12.95

Marijuana Chemistry
Explains the psychoactive constituents of cannabis, and the effect of growth conditions, harvesting, processing and method of ingestion on potency.
199 pgs. photos, illustrations, tables.
HB90 $19.95

Cannabis Alchemy
Revised and updated. The secrets of enhancing potency in this informative text. Extraction and preparation of extremely potent cannabis products.
109 pgs., charts & illustrations.
HB13 $12.95

HIGH TIMES Cultivation Tips
greatest grow guide ever. The best cultivation stories, redaer reports, grow tips and cannabis photos from 20 years of magazines.
124 pgs., photos and illustrations.
HB01 $19.95

Marijuana Botany
Robert Connell Clarke's advanced study on "The Propagation and Breeding of Distinctive Cannabis."
200 pgs., large format, illustrations.
HB46 $19.95

Marijuana: The Cultivator's Handbook
Outdoors, indoors, light, soil, harvest, grafting, nutrients and more.
224 pgs., large format, illustrations and photos.
HB25 $14.95

Gardening: The Rockwool Book
Rockwool gardens yield 10 to 20% more than soil gardens. Complete growing guide.
91 pgs., graphs & photos.
HB89 $14.95

Deluxe Marijuana Grower's Guide
The seminal guide to growing, written by Mel Frank and Ed Rosenthal in 1978 and updated in 1990.
344 pgs.
HB29 $19.95

Marijuana Grower's Insider's Guide
Mel Frank's classic, comprehensive guide for both novice and experienced gardeners.
382 pgs., illustrations and photos.
HB53 $19.95

The Sinsemilla Technique
How to develop seedless female plants.
136 pgs., large format, illustrated.
HB30 $24.95

The Mushroom Cultivator
The definitive reference guide for the home mycologist.
416 pgs., illustrations and photos.
HB37 $29.95

Marijuana Hydroponics: High-Tech Water Culture
BY DANIEL STORM

NEW!
Paradise Burning
Today's world of marijuana: its players and cultivators, its philosophies, its lords and zombies, its growers and smokers, all rolled into a book by HT writer Chris Simunek.
H119 $12.95

Marijuana Hydroponics
Has all the information needed to set up a system using nutrient solutions for growing without soil.
117 pgs., charts, graphs & photos.
HB96 $14.95

HIGH TIMES Greatest Hits: 20 Years of Smoke In Your Face
The greatest collection of HIGH TIMES articles, stories, and tidbits ever collected between two covers. Covers everything from pop culture to pot cultivation, from dope to hemp, from Rockers For Pot to Families Against Mandatory Minimums.
200 pgs., photos and illustrations.
HB99 $13.95

PLEASE SEND ME THE BOOKS I HAVE INDICATED BELOW:

NAME

ADDRESS

CITY STATE ZIP

BOOK #	TITLE	QTY	PRICE	COST

❑ Payment Enclosed* ❑ VISA ❑ MasterCard

SUBTOTAL

Add $1.75 shipping for each book

TOTAL

*Make check or money order payable to: TRANS HIGH

Card#____________

Expiration Date____________

Signature____________

MAIL COUPON WITH PAYMENT ORDER TO:
TRANS HIGH PRODUCTS
PO BOX 621
Mt. Morris, IL 61054

Please allow 6-8 weeks for processing and delivery. TSOG2

BOOKSTORE